This book is dedicated in loving memory of my father-in-law
Madhav Rao…
Whose light shines through every page…

I Remember You
"I remember you in the wings of a bird,
I remember you when dusk turns outward.
I remember you when I give of myself,
I… remember you.
I remember you in the salt of my tears,
I remember you and no longer do I fear.
I remember you in our candle's ray,
I… remember you.
I remember you and do the right thing,
I remember you as the seeds of birth begin.
I remember you in every living beat.
I… will always… remember you."

Samira Rao

"Illness is not cured by saying the word "medicine,"
but by taking medicine. Enlightenment is not achieved by repeating
the word "God" but by directly experiencing God.
Talk as much philosophy as you like, worship as many gods as you
please,
observe ceremonies and sing devotional hymns,
But liberation will never come, even after a hundred aeons,
Without realizing the Oneness".

Sankara

Acknowledgements

I would like to express my admiration and gratefulness to every individual who contributed their story for this book. Many of them I know personally, which makes these stories even more sacred. Some names in this book have been changed in order to maintain the privacy and protection of others.

By listening to their experiences, I have come to recognize the value of God's blessings in my life. By hearing their pain and viewing their tears, I have come to accept what I have taken for granted. By feeling their joy for the small bounty that many would consider treasure-less, I have come to remove the stained glass window that clouded my own truths and emanated synthetic realities.

Table of Contents

Introduction

Growing up, I came from two religious backgrounds, Catholicism and Hinduism. Here, I had the unique opportunity and experience of being embraced by an Eastern and a Western belief system. Having been raised Catholic, but familiar with Hinduism, an awareness and understanding developed in relation to spirituality versus religion.

With Catholicism being the dominant faith in our family; events such as Baptism, Holy Communion, Confession on Sundays, and serving the church as an altar girl were very important. However, within me, I felt a stirring to explore more. My mother, an East Indian Roman Catholic and devoted to her faith, saw her way of devotion as the only form. To this day she attends church regularly and is very devout in her worship. I admire her for that, for she has unearthed an inner peace and contentment through her belief. For myself, having little knowledge of my father's religion left a void, which instilled me to search on.

My mother gave the foundation that every child needs growing up, acknowledgement of mysticism and faith in divinity at an early age. However, growing up, I began to see the three of us, my two brothers and me, venturing onto a different path. Since I can only speak for myself. I felt a yearning to know more about Eastern mysticism and its tenets, not just the various religious symbols that surrounded our home.

My search led me down several pathways of Eastern and Western doctrines. After a quest for the inner truth, I came full circle to embrace both Eastern and Western philosophies of faith. I understood that regardless of our religious ideologies or differing cultures, the realization that permeated within was essence of indivisibility for spirit and love of God. I recognized that by respecting the universality of religions, hence, different truths, we are one step closer to Self-mastery.

I would like to quote a story from Joseph Campbell's audio collection, *The Power of Myth* that elicits what I hope will capture in you, when reading these thoughts.

"Joseph Campbell was in Japan for a conference in religion. He overheard another American delegate, a social philosopher from New York, say to a Shin-To priest 'we've been now to a good many ceremonies and have seen quite a few of your shrines, but I don't get your ideology, I don't get your theology'. The Japanese paused as

*though in deep thought and slowly shook his head. 'I think we don't have ideology he said, we don't have theology—**we dance***'.

When reading these thoughts, they are not to be dissected as a newspaper report; but preferably, they present another approach to life…*the world behind our minds.* Not all Thoughts correspond with a story. The stories presented here hope to bring a more lucid understanding of a few thoughts expressed.

My intention is not for you to concentrate on the phenomenon of the stories; rather, that you seize some of the lessons these individuals discovered. My wish is for you to focus on the changes that each one mastered and how they now view life.

My aim is that we enlighten ourselves to our surroundings, to the being within each of us, which I believe is the first step to living *present time*. This being may be referred to as the soul, center or spirit, while others may simply label it their individuality.

Reincarnation is one of several concepts discussed in this book. I would like to address the point that if you differ with this conception of thought, to try to keep an open mind. For what remains significant is not whether you agree or disagree with the concept of reincarnation, but how you govern the life you have today. Whichever concepts you follow—believe in the Oneness of you—for only then can the maturation of a stream—flow as a river.

As Sri Sathya Sai Baba writes:

*"We are all One, be alike to everyone. **Worship the God of your choice**. There are many names and forms of God, but He is one. You can be called a son, brother, husband, father, or grandfather and still be the same person with many names. It is the same with God."*

"There is only one Religion, the Religion of Love.
There is only one Language, the Language of the Heart.
There is only one Race, the Race of Humanity.
There is only one God, and He is Omnipresent."
Sri Sathya Sai Baba

****I bestow my love and gratitude to Sri Sathya Sai Baba for imparting in me the inspiration to write this book. I am humbled by his act of twice blessing the manuscript and instilling in me the confidence to see this book through to completion.***

Your Life

"When the time of judgment comes, we shall not be asked what we have read but what we have done."

Swami Chinmayananda

Thought 1

Living in chaos is living in stability? A paradox no doubt, but one of life's many truths.

When an understanding can be reached that life can never be one straight line, that there are times when this line will have its dips and curves; we have then plugged into the enigma of stability versus chaos, which makes life—*livable.*

When we can fully apprehend that chaos is an offshoot of stability and that stability is an offshoot of chaos—only then will we be able to overcome even the most tragic of circumstances. It will become easier to fathom that these two opposites are exactly the same—and that the difference lies within one's own perception.

When this can be appreciated, we have begun the walk of *who we are*.

* * *

This is a story of many women— I am presenting three different perspectives that deal with loss, pain and the capacity to see stability within the chaos.

This is the first of three perspectives.

This is Cassandra's story:

I was blessed with two children—a girl and then a boy. My husband and I decided that we would like another child. Soon after, I thought that I was pregnant. I was getting ready to take a test when I had quite a bit of hemorrhaging and abdominal pain. I went to my obstetrician as I knew that something was definitely wrong. The bleeding became a constant flow. My doctor told me that I had a spontaneous miscarriage and this was very common. At that point I was about six weeks pregnant.

This miscarriage was probably the most emotional for me, as it never occurred in mind that I could miscarry. Both my first and second babies were conceived effortlessly—without actually trying. I guess you could say that I was a little in shock. After this transpired, my husband and I began trying actively to get pregnant. About two months later I conceived. I was about eight weeks pregnant and very excited, however, I decided to keep a low profile in sharing the news. At the ninth week, I had abdominal pains and exceedingly heavy bleeding. My doctor confirmed that it was a miscarriage, as a lot of clotting had occurred.

By this time I began to feel that maybe there was a pattern occurring and that maybe I could not conceive. I remember talking to friends at that time and telling them that I always took for granted that I could have children. I had so many friends that could not get pregnant and who were going through this whole fertility thing—but in my mind I was not one of **those** women. I was a woman who could have babies very easily and never had to try.

And so it was at that time that I began to view this in a whole new perspective—I started to recognize that I might not be able to have another child. For six or seven months we remained off birth control and continued trying. It was then that I had my third miscarriage—I was about three weeks, although very early in the pregnancy it was still a loss. By this time I felt quite sad and hopeless. We decided that we could not get pregnant and went back on birth control. We made a mutual decision that two children was enough, and that we needed to be happy with what we had.

About a year later we moved to another state, as my husband was starting his first job out of residency. I had become quite sick and had swollen glands and abdominal problems for about a month, which I could not shake. I went to see my physician where I conveyed my symptoms. He then palpated my abdomen and said he felt a mass. He told me that I might have abdominal cancer. He said that I should go for an abdominal ultrasound right away. My husband and I were in shock. In my mind, I started planning on how I was going to say good-bye to my children.

The day of the ultra sound I remember the technician saying to me *"Mrs. Lockner, is there any chance that you could be pregnant"?*

The second he said it I could hear this voice screaming in my head saying, *"that's it—my God I am pregnant!"*

But because of the miscarriages for two years I had mentally played this game of hope and disappointment. Thinking that maybe I was pregnant and not being pregnant or maybe I was pregnant—and losing it. So I had gotten into a place where I did not believe my own intuition anymore.

But something in my voice did not sound certain as I turned to the technician and said, *"no, I am absolutely sure that I am not pregnant."*

He said, *"look—you're Dr. Lockner's wife. If I go ahead and radiate your entire abdomen and you are pregnant, I am going to feel really horrible about that. Why don't we take a quick blood test—it will only take ten minutes".*

I said, *"No, no, no—that is a waste of time. Let's not even bother."*

Yet the whole time I was saying this—my sixth sense was screaming, take the pregnancy test. Well, the technician took the blood test and it took about thirty minutes.

The entire while I kept turning to the two technicians saying, *"it won't be positive—there is no way I am pregnant".*

The phone rang and I heard the technician say, *"really—oh really."*

The technician came back in and says, *"well you do have a mass—but it should deliver itself in about seven or eight months."*

I was totally shocked. I left the hospital and suddenly a feeling of certainty emerged, where I knew that this baby would be okay. I never thought I would miscarry nor have any of the complications I had previously. I innately knew this child was going to be born healthy—and it was. I delivered a healthy baby seven and a half months later.

I view my miscarriages as my body's way of making sure that something, which may not have been right, did not happen. I try not to look at the three miscarriages as the babies I should have had. Rather, I try to go beyond and see that possibly these were the babies I was not meant to have at that time. I take these miscarriages as a blessing in disguise, however painful it might have been. For I knew in the very depths of my heart that I was not equipped emotionally to handle a child that may have had some developmental problems if that were to be the case.

In my mind this was a child that was not ready to be born—and my body at that particular time could not connect with the soul of that child. The timing was not right, and possibly the greater good of this was what I was able to learn through these three experiences.

The experience of the miscarriages has given me a sense of humbleness and empathy that I never had before. The part of me that thought of myself as liberal and caring would like to think that I never thought like that—but in retrospect I did. One of my closest friends wanted a third child and had numerous miscarriages in between both children. When she first had trouble conceiving I thought that I had understood—but I didn't really get it. I would tell her how sorry I was—but inside I would think that there was something wrong with her, as conceiving really should not have been a problem. Somewhere inside myself, there was a slightly superior attitude about this whole baby experience.

Whereas when I found myself not conceiving, I realized how out of my control it really was and what an emotional thing to face every month. It changed my view as a woman able to have children. I do not think that it is a given anymore—but a blessing.

I have become more empathetic to other women who are struggling to conceive and are dealing with miscarriages. The miscarriage itself made me look at pregnancy and childbearing differently. Whether you miscarry or cannot conceive, either way you are struggling to have a child. It made me see things through the lens of their eyes and made me feel a part of their anguish. I now really do get it—and I now grasp a little of what it feels to be on the other side.

This is Cindy's story:

I found out that I was pregnant two months before I was to marry my husband. I had mixed emotions, as I had miscarried once before. I felt that I could not lose another baby—I just did not think I had the strength inside to cope with it if it were to happen again. I was to be married August 20, 1994, and on August 3, 1994, I miscarried at eight weeks. It's ironic how things work out, but the strength I thought I never had, came forth. I was able to pull myself together and focus on the life I was about to share with my husband, not the life that I had just lost.

September 18, 1994, we found out that I was pregnant again. The doctor said that I was nearing the eight-week mark. He went on to say that if I were to lose another baby, I would probably not be able to carry anymore.

We had always wanted a big family but now we were praying to just get through this one pregnancy. During the time I was pregnant, I had five laser surgeries on each eye to stop me from going blind. Having been an anorexic for seven years, I grew a lot of excess blood vessels in the back of my eyes and when I became pregnant the excess volume was so great that they were rupturing. The doctors had to coagulate them to save my sight. It was an extremely difficult pregnancy, as I had numerous infections that caused me to go into several episodes of pre-term labor. Alexis was born six weeks premature and was placed in Neonatal ICU. After four days, she was released and is now a very healthy little girl.

About a month before I was to deliver, the doctors told me that having any more children would put my health at great risk. They said that alongside all my previous complications and being a diabetic, another pregnancy might induce kidney failure. I had an emergency C-section, and right after her birth I had a tubal ligation. I went into a depression for quite awhile—as this surgery made it final that I could no longer bear children.

After a few months of deep introspection, I asked myself if it was worth it to go through this kind of pain. Precious time was being lost with my husband and daughter. I began to tell myself that I needed to start appreciating the here and now—and to stop dwelling in my sadness. I had a beautiful seven-month old daughter and a wonderful husband — how bad was my life really?

My husband and I then talked about adoption. I told him that I did not want to go through a normal adoption procedure, as it would take forever—and that there were so many children out there that needed a good home right now, at this moment. We then made the decision to adopt a child who was developmentally disabled. My mother and sisters tried to talk us out of it.

I remember one conversation where my mom said to me, *"you don't want to do this—you really don't want to do this. Why can't you be satisfied with what you have."*

I told her, *"I am satisfied with what I have—but that does not mean that I cannot have another child."*

My mother can usually talk me out of most things—but this was one subject I felt very strongly about. I can't explain it, but I just knew that there was a child out there waiting to come home. I just knew that this child had a really horrible life. In my heart I felt there was a reason that I could not have another child biologically, and that there was another soul out there who had to go through another woman to get to its real home.

We finally got placed with one child named Richard, but it fell through. I remember talking to the lady who was our child-finder (a person that works with a couple to find a child) and she said that I should not give up, that there was a reason why God chose not to give this child to me at this time. But my husband and I decided to give it up as it became too emotional, especially with the last one falling through. I guess you can say that I left it up to the Universe—I surrendered.

We got a call two months later from our child-finder saying, *"how about a two year old red headed boy?"*

The first thing I asked was, *"what is the matter with him"*.

After the fall out with baby Richard, I wanted to know up front how severely disabled this child was. I did not want to find out later what I should have been told before I made the commitment.

She said, *"well, I will get with his social worker and see if he will send you any information."*

As soon as she said that, I instantly knew that our wait was over. I hung up the phone with an overwhelming sense that this little boy was ours. This insight arose an inner peace that I had never experienced. It was then that I knew that this was the little soul we were waiting for. This voice that would always push me not to give up—suddenly quieted—and a new voice emerged, which told me to get ready, as he was coming sooner than we thought.

From that day on everything went so smoothly. We had to pinch ourselves to make sure we were not dreaming. From his social worker to the child's foster mother, we received all the information necessary for us to make an informed decision. We found out that Scott's biological parents were drug addicts. And due to his mother taking drugs all through her pregnancy Scott had cerebral palsy. He also had four other siblings who were adopted—and his mother was pregnant again.

Everything just flowed—there were no more obstacles, Scott became part of our family when he was 2 1/2 years old. It is so ironic how things work out because he was the spitting image of my husband. They look so much alike that it is uncanny.

Looking back I would do this all over again in an instant. I believe that Scott was ours from the time he was born. I do not regret having my tubes tied or not being able to conceive another child biologically. There was a plan already in the making—long before even I was aware of it. And once I surrendered—the pieces of the puzzle fell into place.

This is Lydia's story:

My husband and I married in 1989 and in 1992 decided to start a family. We became pregnant rather quickly and throughout the duration of the first pregnancy there were no complications. I am a physician and was able to work up until the day I delivered. I took calls up until two weeks before my delivery date. I nursed my son for about a year and then we tried actively for almost a year to have another baby.

Unsuccessful in conceiving, I went ahead and had a hysterosalpingogram done on me, which was a test where dye is injected into your tubes to see if they are opened. The hysterosalpingogram was normal and the following month I became pregnant. I started having some very early spotting that continued off and on. I was having ultrasounds very frequently and despite the spotting the baby was fine.

One night the spotting turned into significant bleeding but I had no abdominal cramping. The next morning the cramping began and I was passing large clots. I knew I was miscarrying and went to my doctor's office with an attitude of preparing myself to see the fetus on ultrasound with no fetal heartbeat. At my doctor's, I was feeling a pressure sensation, I was about to go to the bathroom when the nurse stopped me and told me to wait for the doctor. So, I laid back down on the examining table.

Shortly thereafter, the doctor came in and upon examining me found that the fetus was in the vagina. It was fully formed at four months. I was not prepared to see what I saw, I was expecting to view my baby on the ultrasound monitor and not in my physician's hands. My doctor took the fetus out and I saw my baby's legs hanging from her cupped hands. I was devastated. I found out that it was a girl.

Soon after, I began thinking that things could be worse. I could have gone full term only to give birth to a stillborn child. I had one biological baby and it was a lot more than other women had. When I was pregnant with Kevin, it was a wonderful experience and I loved every moment of that pregnancy. I would look forward to seeing my baby on the ultrasound and feeling his kick within me. These were a few of the many thoughts I focused on after the first miscarriage. I kept telling myself that yes, I had a miscarriage—but life could be a lot worse—and is a lot worse for many other people.

We began trying a few months later for a little over six months. At that point, I was thirty-five and decided to see a fertility expert. We tried fertility drugs with insemination for several cycles. All attempts were unsuccessful. It became an emotional roller coaster to say the least.

We then decided to do in-vitro fertilization. At the retrieval time, they obtained ten good eggs which fertilized. They transferred five embryos and froze the remaining five embryos. Approximately twelve days later, I found out that I was pregnant. We were thrilled. A few weeks later we were told that they were twins. The first three months were fine—I became very attached to the babies as I saw them growing on the ultrasound. Due to the nature of the pregnancy, ultrasounds were done mostly every week. I had some spotting early on, but it stopped and the doctor was not too concerned.

I began my second trimester and all was well. I was in my fourth month when all of a sudden I started running a fever. I began to take Tylenol and initially the fever subsided. However, it continued for about three days. Before long, I began to experience discomfort in the right side of the lower abdomen. I thought for a brief moment that it might be appendicitis but the pain didn't seem severe enough. Then I began to spot and knew at that point that I might be miscarrying. I went to the perinatologist office where I was scheduled to have an amniocentesis and told them what symptoms were occurring.

They did an ultrasound, which showed that the babies were fine. They sent me to the emergency room for evaluation of the fever, right lower abdominal pain and vaginal bleeding. They thought that it might be appendicitis, as my white blood cell count was high, alongside a fever and abdominal pain. They kept me overnight. By midnight the bleeding became quite heavy and I began cramping. I felt at this point that I was in possible labor. It was very frightening being alone. I called my husband at 3:00 a.m. and he rushed over. By this point, I was having pretty strong contractions and knew that my twins were more or less not going to make it. After about 5 1/2 hours of being in labor, they finally gave me a shot of Demerol for the pain. I remember wanting to go to the bathroom, but restrained from going, as I was afraid that the babies would come out.

After 5 1/2 hours of wanting to go to the bathroom but holding off, I went with a nurse. My fears came true as the first baby passed through and was hanging by its umbilical cord in the toilet. The nurse quickly wrapped the fetus in a sheet, as I walked back to my bed with the umbilical cord attached to me while she was holding my baby. My doctor then came in and removed the first baby. The second baby was in the vagina area and he removed it. The nurse wrapped and brought both babies to me to hold and say good-bye. I touched and held my twin boys and then let them go on.

For the next few months I concentrated on healing and focusing on the things I had in life, rather than what I did not have. A good friend of mine sent me a prayer of St. Jude and said that she was praying to him that I might be blessed with one more baby. I took comfort that my friend was directing her thoughts and prayers to me, and I accepted what she gave with an open heart.

It becomes very easy to dwell in the anguish and remain steadfast in its energy. I believe no matter how hard our perception of suffering is, there are still things that one can get up in the morning and enjoy no matter how terrible we feel. I had a beautiful son at home who needed my love and attention. Walking in the mornings became like a meditation—it allowed me to reflect, release and refocus. Every morning I looked forward to just Being, in my walking.

A few months later, we thawed the remaining five embryos and transferred the four surviving ones inside me. It did not take and I did not get pregnant. About a couple of months later, we decided to try IVF one more time before considering the idea of adoption. The pregnancy test prior to the drugs was negative. I began taking Lupron, which decreases your estrogen prior to taking the follicle stimulating drugs. In some cases the estrogen rises before it falls.

After about two weeks of being on the Lupron, my estrogen level was not falling. The doctor ordered a double dosage of Lupron for me to inject myself with. Due to my rising level, I did not take the double dosage even though the nurse said that it in some women the estrogen level rises before it falls. Call it a gut instinct or my intuition working overtime, but I decided to get a home pregnancy test first, before I went ahead. The same pregnancy test I was doing for five years that always turned out negative, came back positive when I least expected it to.

Before I could even contemplate this pregnancy, my main concern was the intake of Lupron I had been injecting for two weeks and the effect it would have on the baby and my pregnancy. I called my physician in a panic. He said that if the Lupron did anything the result would be a possible miscarriage. I went for an ultrasound. We could not see or detect a fetus at first. I mentally began preparing myself for another miscarriage. However, subsequent ultrasounds did show a live fetus. I was then referred to a perinatologist, who followed me through my entire pregnancy. Nine months later, I gave birth to a very healthy seven-pound baby girl, whom we named Savannah.

By focusing on what I had in life—it really kept me from hitting rock bottom. And when I felt like I had hit bottom, well— I embraced it—and allowed myself to feel that way. I believe our time on this planet is too precious to remain in our pain. I take the time to savor in the simplicity that life brings me. For in simplicity there is freedom. And it is through these simple moments that I am most appreciative and grateful for the blessings I have had and continue to have in my life.

Thought 2

If you were asked this question, 'what have you done with your life'? How would you answer? If you were asked this question, 'what have you accomplished with the precious time you have been allotted'? How would you answer? Are you able to go beyond your immediate interests and Self-gratification; or was it mostly about you, your family and your accomplishments?

Think about this question with some thought, before you try to respond. Remember this question does not encompass how young or old you are, nor does it focus on what you did not have in life. Rather, it pertains to what did you do with what you did have.

It is in the act of letting go that one is able to love. It is in the act of releasing life that one can then begin to live in it.

Thought 3

Recognizing that our life here on this plane is limited to an allotted number of years—why then do many of us waste much of our time *living in fear?* Why is it that some of us first put our faith into living *limited* rather than living *limitless*?

To live a limited life is to live within the boundaries of the five senses, unable to go beyond and sensitize who we are to the Universe and its surroundings. A limited individual cannot comprehend beyond scientific proof—as his/her lines of thinking are established by society. They tend to live in the arrogance of their intellect, where reason and rationality are the periphery of their cognizance.

When engaging in the sense of limitation—they engage in the sense of accumulation. A limited person accumulates; whether it is success, recognition, power, material possessions, or money— they seem to never have enough.

This accumulation is based on fear that may have stemmed from upbringing, experience or environment. We should all strive to be successful in whatever we choose with our life. However, we must caution against how we implement that success and how *attached* we become to the residue that success may harvest.

There is nothing wrong in living a comfortable life while maintaining a relationship that is close to God and earth. We can enjoy all the luxuries that success brings and yet maintain a sense of Self and spirituality, by not allowing the Self to become *defined* and *bound* to its fruits.

Thought 4

There comes a point in one's life where the need to know why things have happened the way they have, become insignificant. There comes a time when the answers to the *"why me or the what if"* questions will never be explained.

These are some of life's mysteries that cannot be solved. In due time, the very answers we are looking for are the ones that will never be known—that in itself becomes our answer. Sometimes, not all of life's complexities are for us to comprehend—from time to time, the answer lies in living it.

Thought 5

Learning to love our shadow Self— is like learning to love the uncomfortable and insecure components of what we are. To realize our Oneness we must unite both Selves. This is the first step in becoming whole and is easier said then done. By confronting the parts we mask to the outside world, we can begin to look at who we really are— and not at what we think we are. To do this is to embrace humility, and when one embraces humility, one embraces acceptance.

Projection is one of the first signs of our shadow Self. Projection can be seen at the individual or group level. Recognizing what we dislike in others can shed light on our own reflection. Disintegration of the shadow takes the embracing of what we have rejected and denied in the past. In situations where feelings of unpleasantness are generated, it is our shadow Self clamoring to be recognized. This is where we must turn inward and acknowledge our own characteristics rather than projecting our dislikes and pettiness on to others. This act ignites the path of initiation.

Thought 6

It is easy to forget what's important. It's easy to be swayed away in the current of life's tide. Work, for many of us, is a necessity. However, when it becomes too consuming and we find ourselves always in a hurry, this no longer remains a sign but becomes a red flag warning.

We must not wait until the very end to appreciate *the here and now*. Regrets will be just that—regrets. Many of us will leave this plane of existence wishing we had lived differently, wishing perhaps that we had spent more quality time with our loved ones, or realizing how much energy was wasted towards petty worry, blame, and needless anger.

Therefore, when you find the need to be continually occupied and boredom renders you easily, it is time to become aware of your inner world. One of the first steps is through meditation. It is through meditation that our intuition opens, and it is through meditation that one becomes aware of the mystical presence within each of us.

Ignorance is cultivated when we walk wearing shades—instead of lenses. It is within life's subtleties that divinity helps pave our way, it is within life's subtleties that we are shown a more suitable course. Our journey need only become easier, if we learn to receive their clues with a mind whose receptors are clear from static.

Thought 7

How can one maintain free will and still have destiny? Destiny implies that a plan is implemented since birth. So how is it possible to become what you want in life, while simultaneously having your life predetermined? The answer lies in *choice.*

Destiny implies that our soul may have created choices before we incarnated. Through these choices, circumstances made it possible that certain people and events will transpire in our life. However, this is where destiny ceases and free will governs.

How we react to the people in our life and the situations that we find ourselves confronted by will determine the path we are to follow. Free will is stronger than any other force within or around us.

As we surrender the gates within us to the divine—His consciousness will blend with ours, making His will our will. This, in turn, steers our destiny, carves our choices, and enables the Higher Self to flow through with much more ease. This freedom allows us to choose without having to perceive that a choice was made.

Thought 8

Maintaining a sense of control in life is what many of us strive to accomplish in our daily lives. Many individuals deem it difficult to let the Universe do the worrying but everything, in its own time, has its own answer. The first step to holding the reins in our hands—is by letting them go.

To secure control in a life that increasingly augments chaos—we must first learn to give it up. It is in the act of rendering control that one retains it. We are most in control when we are not. We are most in command—when in surrender. However, this does not imply surrendering without Self-effort!

Thought 9

Obstacles are opportunities in disguise. It may not seem so at that time, but in due course the very hurdle that seemed so unfair and futile is what brought you onto another path. It is the makeup of who you are at this present moment and increases the strength to continue on. The ground that you stand on today is the foundation laid for your tomorrow.

Thought 10

We need to realize that there are no wrong choices, only misplaced attitudes behind our decisions. Being bound to a bad attitude is our mistake. Conversely, there are no wrong choices if wisdom is derived.

Think of this thought as tuition paid—in the school of life.

Thought 11

Suicide may seem the final for many lost individuals, *but is it*? We choose circumstances before coming to this plane of life in order to evolve our growth. When life is cut before its destined time, the soul or spirit does not suddenly "feel different". The problems and suffering brought forth before death will remain in the next plane ~ only this time they will become aware of why those experiences were necessary.

It is not possible to kill yourself; it is only possible to shed ones physical body. In leaving the body, we simply exchange one form for another. Through death there can be only birth, however, whatever problems drove us to suicide will only be relearned in a future cycle and time.

* * *

I hope this story will inspire many to seek help and know that suicide is not the solution. I hope those looking to find a release from their pain on Earth will realize that the answers were always here and never somewhere else. Here is a dear friend's story of her experience with suicide.

This is Casey's story:

My depression and thoughts of suicide started around age thirteen and lasted until I was twenty-four. I always felt different in my family—I always felt out of place. Although I came from a loving home, I felt somewhat like a foreigner.

The time when things fell out of control was in September 1994. I was a manager for a local bookstore when I had a nervous breakdown at work. Stock was piled to the ceiling and there was too much going on in the store for my new co-worker and I to attend to. It was at that point that I ended up calling our employee assistance hotline for help. I must have sounded quite unsettled, as the person at the employee assistance hotline asked me if I thought I could harm myself.

Distressed and overwhelmed, I replied, *"if there was a semi-truck coming through the room I would make sure that I was standing right in front of it."*

The woman handed the telephone to a counselor and immediately an appointment was set up for the same day.

I was three hours late for my appointment, as I ended up getting lost. I landed at the therapy office a mess. I was sitting on the floor with my arms around my knees, rocking back and forth. The therapist asked me if there was anything that she could do for me. I asked her if she had a gun. She of course replied no and wanted to admit me into the hospital right away. I have a fear of hospitals and so we came to an agreement that if I got on medication that day, she would put me on leave.

In order to go on leave at work, one must be admitted to a hospital or go on medication. A psychiatrist friend of hers owed her a favor, and she got me an appointment for that same day.

I told him the story and at the end of it he said, *"Well, what do you want me to do?"*

I said, *"I need medication to go on sick leave, I cannot be at work right now, I need to get away."*

He said, *"Well, I do not know what you want me to do."* I said, *"Listen—I am sick of the crap that I am going through, if you do not want to help fine; but if I walk out that door right now and blow my brains out it will be on your shoulders—not mine."*

He immediately wrote me a prescription and I was sent home.

At that time, I was living with my boyfriend Mike. He seemed to understand what I was going through and was supportive. I quit work in September because I got another job as a receptionist in a real estate office; I felt that the job situation was the source of my problems. Things seemed to be getting better; I was working part time and going to school. About a month later, I got into a car accident and wrecked my car. That same week I found out that my grandmother was in the hospital and our family did not know if she would make it through the weekend. When Mike returned home from skiing that weekend, I gave him the news about what had happened with my grandmother. He said, *"Why don't you go and visit her?"*

I said, *"I don't have a car"*.

He replied, *"Why don't you ask your parents for money to fix your car."*

We got into our first fight over that, since we had been together a year and a half. At the end of the fight I said, *"What do you want me to do— move out?"*

He replied, *"Now that you mentioned it— yes. I can't see you anymore, you are depressed and up and down all the time."*

I was distraught. I did not know what to do. My parents came to pick me up and I cried the entire way home, as my mom held me. Mike still wanted to see me, but he insisted that I needed to change things about myself. He wanted me to lose weight, eat better and concentrate on school more. It seemed that there was a constant need for me to change this or that. I just kept saying to myself that he was right; I will just do this all for him. A month later, he ended telling me that he hated me and continued on to say that he did not want to see me again. I was in torment all over again.

The next day, March 20, 1995, was extremely fuzzy to me. I remember getting up, taking a shower and getting dressed for work. I remember standing in front of the medicine cabinet that we have in our kitchen. I don't remember grabbing anything. All I can recall is looking at my hands and seeing a bunch of pills of different colors and sizes. I did not know whose they were, or where they came from. I kept thinking that this was my way out. I believed that I would not ever have to deal with this again. I just wanted it to end. I remember taking two handfuls of pills and swallowing three glasses of water. I laid on the couch, all dressed up in my skirt and blouse, *ready to die.*

While lying there, I thought to myself, I do not want to die alone, but I do not want someone to save me either. The only person I could think of calling who would not have a choice but to listen to me was Matt, a very dear friend of mine, who lived in Texas. He is usually never home, but when I tried that morning, he answered.

We talked about my breakup, as he knew I was going through a hard time. Within seconds, I started having a hard time breathing; it seemed that each breath was a struggle. I started feeling my legs and thighs going numb. I thought to myself, wow this is good; the pain is starting to go away. The difficulty was in the breathing, which became rather strenuous.

After a few more breaths, it got increasingly difficult to speak; it was then that I confided in Matt about what I had done. The first thing he told me was to hang up and call 911. I told him no.

He then said to call his mother, or his family's pastor, he said *" just call someone...please don't kill yourself."*

I told him *"I can't, I just want to die."*

He tried to convince me to call someone, but soon he came to the realization that I was not going to do anything to save myself. It was almost like the calm before the storm.

He quite suddenly composed himself and he said, *"O.K, you know I am here for you".*

Then he said, *"I miss you."*

I requested him to tell my parents that it was not their fault. He said that he would.

He kept saying *"I love you... do not leave me... you are a wonderful human being... just don't leave like this, I need you."* I told him I was feeling sick and in a calm voice he said, *"good...go throw up."*

Almost like a subliminal message he kept reiterating, *"make yourself sick".*

Then he would add, *"I love you"*, then repeat *"make yourself sick...I need you"*...and again... *"make yourself sick... do not leave me."* He was reinforcing what I needed to hear. The last thing he said to me before we hung up was, "*te amo"* (I love you in Spanish).

It was a special word that we shared. I do not know if it triggered something in my brain, but I hung up and vomited.

I ended up going to work, where I told my boss what had just transpired. She immediately got on the telephone and contacted my parents. I came home with my father and as we pulled up into our driveway, my mother ran out of the house and gave me a heart-wrenching hug.

My mom was already on the phone to various psychiatrists and health clinics, trying frantically to find some place for me to get in. I thought my parents would start to run my life, although I knew they would do what was best at that time. It truly amazed me when my mother posed different types of options that I needed to consider.

It became very hard to find a psychiatrist; most were booked for months. My mother and I decided to go to Family Catholic Services, where we went through a number of therapists. The only way that they allowed me not to be hospitalized was if my mother volunteered to watch me twenty-four hours a day. She did and with that took time off work. Through this, all I could do was imagine having a child of my own going through something similar. This is what she was dealing with day in and day out.

There came a point when I had enough and did not want to put my parents through any more of my messed up life. I made a decision to leave. I recall feeling that I was never going to find a psychiatrist. With each day passing, I was more overwhelmed. The pain was not going away, it was getting worse. My mom asked me where I was going and I told her that I did not want to do this to her and dad anymore. I told her I needed to get out.

She kept saying, *"No, you are our daughter, we love you, we want to get you through this."*

My mother stood between my car and me. I said to her, *"get out of my way"*.

She replied, *"I can't let you go."*

I looked at my mother and said, *"Mom, this is the last thing I want to do, but if you don't move I am going to hit you."*

I have never hit my mother, I would not dream of touching my parents.

My mother looked me straight in the eye as she let go of both my hands and said, *"You give me your best shot baby...because I love you."*

I fell down on my knees and cried, as she fell down on her knees and held me. Something deep inside triggered off hope, where I knew at that point that I had something to live for. I realized then, that what I was doing was not going to end my pain—it was only going to prolong it.

I went back to school after being off for two weeks and informed my professors of what was going on. One of my professors directed me to a psychiatrist in the Detroit area. She called him and an appointment was scheduled in three days. She even went to his office on Saturday to meet with my parents and me; she was a special lady who cared. She was there when I needed to unburden myself in and out of her classroom.

I had sessions with this psychiatrist for two months, twice a week. He told me that I was not crazy and that I should allow myself to feel what I am feeling. He went on to say that suicide was not the answer, but that I had to resolve my problems. Suicide was not going to take it away; it was only going to end my physical life—not my mental life. As long as I was not resolving my problems here, it would plague me someplace else. He told me that my body was simply a capsule—only a shell. He said that inside me lived a wonderful person waiting to live and experience life.

It was through him that I found out that I had a chemical imbalance in my brain. He put me on the proper medication that I needed. Soon afterward, I was referred to a psychiatrist and therapist closer to home. To this day, I still receive support.

I now give speeches for therapy classes and high schools; I have even communicated to various people on the Internet going through similar predicaments. I will soon obtain my degree in Organizational Communications, I hope to one day assist in developing employee assistance programs in various businesses, like the one that helped me.

I have learned to take one day at a time. I have realized that each moment in our life is so precious. I realize now—what little planet time we truly have. Everyday I wake up and take a moment to thank God for the wonderful life he has given me. I appreciate listening to the birds sing. I appreciate waking up to my family's morning rituals, like the clanging of pots and pans, and the perking of the coffee machine. I am learning daily the meaning of loving the Self inside of me. I am learning daily about loving my life in just the package that it came in. I do not lose hope anymore, for I now realize that I was always home.

Thought 12

We are a life system of balance and imbalance. What suicide creates is an imbalance in our soul through actions where the intent behind the action is inappropriate. When we terminate life due to fear, despair, guilt, or any emotion that emulates disparity, we disrupt a life pattern set forth before we agreed to incarnate.

Through karma we have a chance to restore healing in our life system by choices that will bring about balance and empowerment within each of our souls nucleus. These pathways that God provides enable us to facilitate different opportunities, whereby the process of mending can commence.

These opportunities may not mean one will relive the exact circumstance. Its appearance may present itself as a healer to those contemplating suicide, or enduring the strength in this life to surpass and overcome hardships, rather than shorten life before its destined time. Whatever path we partake, if we have the strength to overcome, it will realign and equilibrate what we have done to Self.

Thought 13

We live in a world where many of us find ourselves caught up with external channels. These channels emerge in the facets of alcohol, work, smoking, eating disorders, compulsive spending, and any other type of addiction that one finds difficult to unplug from.

Why is it that despite the effects it has on the trilogy of mind-body-spirit, we continue to crave them? Why is it that a drink, cigarette, or the need to purchase something in order to uplift spirits is required? What drives our inner essence into evaporation and our power into a reality that is but—a maya (illusion)?

If we are to look deeply into the mirror that shines back at us, we will find that it is our sense of ego, which determines our sense of perception. We will come to understand that the emptiness that pervades our existence is not filled in these conduits, but in our weaknesses. And then we will look away—hoping to see something other than who we are. For it is in these externals that life is easier to contend with. It is in these externals that instant gratification is met.

However, it is within the 'I Am', our center of consciousness that balance manifests. And it is in this center where our authentic nature dwells. Expressions of unhappiness and instability arise when the center is pulled from its core and plugged outwardly.

Thought 14

Procrastination, we all do it, but some are avid scholars at the job. One of the biggest obstacles for many is forming a routine in the spiritual arena. Think how important it is to be on time at your work. Day in and day out you make the deadline for walking in on time. Why is that? Fear of losing your job or not getting that next promotion may be some of the reasons. Whatever the rationale, you make it a priority.

Now, imagine if you knew how important the internal world was to your daily existence within your family environment, work arena, and social network. Would it then become a priority?

If it did, we would see a massive resurgence in our world's consciousness. Lack of duality will take form as we submerge ourselves in getting to know our Self. This acknowledgement will then churn our perspectives into uncovering how un-separate we are from each other. And then, the only illusion created will come from our own lack of limitation and awareness.

Remember, everything we have is left behind at death; our soul, which is filled with knowledge and Samskaras, (past actions) are the only parts that carries on.

Acceptance, not Toleration

"Always try to put yourself in the position of the other and judge your action against that background. Then you will not be wrong."

Sri Sathya Sai Baba

Thought 15

The very attributes that you dislike in another sometimes turn out to be the very ones that mirror *you.* Particularly, if you find yourself speaking often about those individuals and are easily irritated by their behavior. Ask yourself why? Why do you spend your energy in negative talk or judgment of another? Why do you permit your power to deplete in theirs? Deliberately learn to remove yourself from the situation or master the insight to see beyond it, possibly looking at its innocence.

It is a waste of one's thought forms to engage precious time voicing negativity about another and sad when some delight is found in doing so. We all have a choice to live today like it is our only day (*which it is*). So why waste a moment building unfavorable energies and thoughts around ourselves? What inevitably materializes from such actions are that the same energies we put into the Universe will multiply back to us, resulting in like begets like.

Thus, the type of people that surround our lives are usually attracted to us by the energetic vibrations we furnish internally and externally. So, if you are a person with little empathy for others, you might find yourself to be around people of like nature, possibly finding yourself in a situation that calls for empathy and not receiving it. If you are someone who does not think twice about lending a hand, the people in your life will reflect that same energy pattern.

I have come to realize through my own inner work that when I allowed myself to be affected by certain persons, it was partly due to weaknesses that remained dormant within me. Take a good look at who you are before commenting on another. *Maybe you will recognize that you were not so different after all.*

Thoughts 16

Don't waste time thinking about the nice things that would put a smile on another's face—do it! The vibration of the act will multiply onto others through the metaphysical laws of universal karma.

Therefore, however small or inconsequential an action may seem to you, do not hesitate to implement it. Put your initial thought into execution! In the end, what will be remembered is not the act itself, but the sweet residue that lingered from it.

* * *

This story comes from a colleague of my husband. In the process of losing her mother, Judi gains insight into the core meaning of empathy.

This is Judi's story:

My parents moved from Florida to Michigan in July 1998 to be closer to their children and grandchildren. My sisters and I were looking forward to having our parents live near by. We thought it would be a nice few years where our children would be able to get to know their grandparents a little better.

In November 1998, my mother started complaining that she was not feeling well. She did not have much of an appetite and was losing weight. My mother is a very petite person and a ten pound loss showed up immediately on her. She felt bloated in the stomach region. When I examined her there, she looked like she was four to five months pregnant. As a physician, I knew there was something seriously wrong. I said to my mom that she would have to go to her doctor and have this checked out. She called up her physician and a CAT scan was scheduled.

I called up the Radiology department at the hospital where she was being treated. I knew the staff as I had done my residency training at this hospital. I spoke with the resident on duty and asked him to read the results to me. I told him that I knew there was something wrong. I did not want the results unread for several days or lost under a pile of other work. I had a strong sense that time was of the essence in her case.

The following day I drove to my parents' place. They had not heard from their doctor, so I called up and asked for the report. The physician said there was a large amount of free fluid in her abdomen and a tumor in her pelvis. The lining of her abdomen, which is usually a thin lining, had thickened and small nodular deposits were resting on it. At this point, we did not know if it was benign. In my experience reading CATs it sounded malignant, as benign tumors usually do not appear in the manner this physician described.

My folks were sitting at the dining table while I was on the phone. When I got off, their expressions were earnest and anxious. They quickly asked me what the doctor said. Well, how do you tell your parents what you really suspect and simultaneously give them hope? Instead, I relayed that there was a tumor in mom's abdomen with some free fluid, which appeared abnormal. I told my parents that the doctors wanted to do some testing. They wanted to draw some fluid out, analyze it and see what it might be.

My parents then asked, *"is it cancer"?*

I said, *"we do not know,"* even though I was sure that it was.

My father became teary-eyed while my mother came over to him, put her hand on his hand and said, *"well pop, we're not yet done fighting this, whatever it takes—I am going to fight it".*

My mother had always been the eternal optimist. She had successfully fought two bouts of cancer in her colon and breast. She went through surgery and radiation and survived for ten years. From this mindset she was set for one more round of victory.

I was working the night shift that day, so I had to leave my parents' place soon after the news. I could not help but weep all the way to the hospital, as I knew this was grave. While crying and driving, the song "Angel" by Sarah Maclachlan came on the radio. That song seemed like a Godsend. It helped to place some clarity into what I was feeling and experiencing. I knew at that moment that I must leave it in the arms of an angel. I asked God to do what was best. We could pray for a cure and have the faith that she will survive, or we could surrender and leave it for divinity to do what was best and do what was in the highest good for all concerned.

By mid December, my mother went through the test where fluid was drawn out of her abdomen. The results came back as malignant, but they did not know if it was colon, breast, or ovarian cancer. The issue became either a new ovarian tumor or something that had reoccurred from one of her other cancers. We then had to go to the oncologist. All of this happened before Christmas, so it was quite difficult to be scheduled in. We were registered for an appointment in January.

On Christmas Eve I was hosting dinner at my house. My mother had become terribly nauseated and was vomiting. I prayed silently to God to give her this Christmas. We called the doctor and he prescribed something for her nausea, but voiced to us that if she gets any worse we would have to bring her to the hospital. I just kept praying to God to bestow this Christmas to her and allow her take pleasure from it, if it were to be her last. A few minutes later her vomiting stopped and her feeling of nausea disappeared. She was able to come over and enjoy the dinner, be with us and take part in opening the gifts. The next day she went over to my sister's and relished in their celebration as well without a tinge of feeling unwell.

Shortly after Christmas we went to see the oncologist. I really had to insist that she be seen now, as they were giving me dates for the middle of January. I was in the office with the oncologist and my mother. He was trying to figure out whether it was ovarian cancer or something else without going ahead and doing surgery. The oncologist that we were dealing with was more focused with the clinical aspects of the disease analyzing what it was, rather then what needed to be done. As we were in the office, I began thinking that something needed to be done immediately, because my mother was rapidly losing weight and deteriorating before my eyes.

Finally after going back and forth and doing some further testing, I said to the oncologist that she would never survive surgery due to her fragile condition and age. I said that as a physician, I have seen people go through surgery while many end up in ICU on a ventilator due to a number of causes. Let's just do some chemo and see if it will help. If it doesn't— it doesn't, but at least we know we tried.

They started chemotherapy and everything went topsy turvy—she was dying before our eyes. She could not eat, began vomiting, had diarrhea and her electrolytes and fluids were all off. My father had called me one day in February, as my mother could not control her bowels and in her confused state walked into the closet instead of the bathroom. We took her back to the oncologist and they ended up admitting her to the hospital as she was too dehydrated. She stayed in the hospital for two weeks until she was stabilized. Her oncologist never came once to see her. There were other oncologists who saw her, but the one that we were dealing with never showed up. I kept calling his office and his secretary would tell me that he was not on call at that hospital, and I would have to speak with the attending physician on duty that day. We never knew when the doctors were coming and more importantly, they were not familiar with her history. They would look to see if her sodium was up or down and view all the lab figures, but not look at *her* and her health care for the long term.

We brought my mother home and arranged round the clock care with my other two sisters and myself who lived in the area. By early March of 1999, the situation became worse. She could not get out of bed and I thought that she might not even survive that week. I spoke with my dad and told him that we may need to get hospice care, as mom may not be able to take chemotherapy anymore. Our priority at this point was for our mother to be comfortable and take whatever fulfillment she could in her final months on earth. The Hospice people were there not only to physically support and take care of my mother, but also to support our family and help my mother and us go through the process of death and dying. This part was essential to my father. For a long time, he held on to the hope that the chemotherapy would take care of my mother and things would turn around. He did not want to come to terms with the fact that she was not going to survive.

My parents were married almost fifty years when my mother became sick. I knew my father was always a good person, but if one could have witnessed the devotion that transpired between them and the care he showered on her—it almost became heartbreaking. My dad would put his head down on her pillow and pat my mother telling her that he missed and loved her. She would respond by saying she loved him more then he would ever know. My dad who never cooked or nursed in his life, was now changing my mother's diapers, bathing, and feeding her every day. He did it with such tenderness that towards the end, when her time was drawing near, he told her that he wished that they had more time together.

The day that she passed on, I went to her room and told her that I loved her and not to worry about me as I would be fine. Ever since my divorce, she worried that I did not have someone to take care of me, like she had with my dad. Everyone but my dad said goodbye to my mother. My dad was having a hard time changing his mindset and finding the words in his heart to let her go on.

The chaplain then came out and said, *"John you need to say goodbye. You need to tell her that you are going to be O.K. because she is worried about you. You are the main person she is worried about and holding on for"*.

He then put his head down on the pillow and said, *" Mary, I will be O.K.—the girls will take care of me"*.

My father then kissed her and gently stroked her cheek.

The chaplain then said something that was very comforting for me.

She said, *"the angels are here in this room— they are just waiting for the nod from God on this holy ground"*.

To me that was the most comforting thing said, as it gave me the peace I needed and brought me back to that song I had heard on the radio months back. We sisters Patti, Jackie, and I were in and out of her room as it was too difficult to see her struggle for every breath. My sister in New Jersey was trying to get a flight in. She called about 4:00 p.m. and said she should arrive by 7:30 p.m.

So, my sister Jackie went over to mom and said, *" Jeannie is on her way in, and she is thinking of you"*.

Shortly after, I decided to go to my own home, which was a half a mile away to pack a few things so that I could stay overnight. I thought we might have a few more hours and Jeannie and I could sit with mom. My father went in to shave which is right next to her bedroom and Patti and Jackie were in the living room. A few minutes had elapsed when Jackie went in to check on my mom and found out that she had passed on. Her eyes were wide open and her pupils were dilated. She was looking straight up through the ceiling, as if she saw something beyond what life is here on earth. She had such a look of peace and exhilaration. There was a lack of effort in her expression, all the pain and struggling seemed to dissipate— it appeared as if she had found freedom.

I have been told that sometimes our loved ones wait until they are alone to pass on. The entire day someone was present in her room, except for those five minutes in the early evening when no one was around. I think she must have known that everyone had said good-bye. The interesting part of this is that at 4:00 p.m. we told my mother that Jeannie was on her way from New Jersey. Jeannie was the one person whom she really never got a chance to say good-bye to. My mother passed on at 4:45 p.m. I believe that once she realized that Jeannie was on her way to Michigan, it gave her the comfort and peace that she needed to go on in her journey. I felt that she knew Jeannie would be with us in our circle of love and that it was okay for her to move ahead.

Through my mother's death, I have really learned to appreciate my family. Seeing how my sisters have handled our mother's sickness and the support that was shared between each of us. There was never a day that passed when one of us felt that the other did more or less, we all just did the best we could. As for my father, I truly appreciate his essence spirit and his ability to care for our mother and himself while in great sorrow. He went from someone who did no cooking and light cleaning to taking care of everything and not falling apart in the process.

I am learning to give of myself as my mother did when she was alive. She took life for what it was and appreciated every moment of it—never complained nor asked for much. My mother enjoyed the life she had and the people in it. She was satisfied in Being.

The loss of my mother made me realize how important it is to become more empathetic to others. I can't tell you how much it meant for me when people sent cards, came to the funeral or paid their respects at the funeral home. Before my mother's passing, I was not aware or sensitive enough to other people's pain. With the loss of my own aunts and uncles, I rarely went to the funerals. At my mother's funeral, cousins came whom I had not seen in years, to extend their support and love to all of us. The warm feelings that emanated from their presence became a vital part in sustaining my strength to go on. It shook me up, as I realized that I should have taken the time to go when they were going through their loss.

I guess I could rationalize and say that it was due to my busy schedule as a resident and then attending physician, but this is only self justification. As I look back, I know in my heart that I could have made a little more effort. For myself, I never realized until I went through this process of grieving how unaware and out of touch I was to the feelings of others. One looks back and remembers numerous times that friends or family had gone through similar circumstances and the missed moments in time that a visit, call, or card would have done to aid in their grief.

I now try to emulate this in my own life. I do not wait to walk a mile in another's shoes. Although I may not fully experience or understand what someone has gone through, I try to take the time to delve a little deeper into their pain and their heart.

Thought 17

Become more empathetic. Have patience and kindness to whomever you deem difficult. Find the love and insight to accept and withhold judgment. For God has not delegated authority to you over another's affairs. They might be wrong, but take the time to understand that they are coming from their reality—their own stained glass window.

When you feel the first rise of anger or judgment bubbling in your system, talk to yourself! Internalize a dialogue within your own Self. Consider different possibilities and reasons to help you understand the person your irritation or anger is directed at. This will give you a sense of their perspective.

You may not fully understand their outlook—but by allowing a part of the shutters to remain open, reflection of your soul in some small way will connect to theirs. And by doing so, you will link an element of your thought forms—your vibratory essence—onto theirs.

Thus, by transmitting a particle of your sentience, perforation will take place through their veil of thoughts—leaving seeds to be sown in the depth of their consciousness.

* * *

This story comes from a very dear friend of mine named Anita who lives in Montreal.

This is Anita's story:

One day as I was in a shopping mall, I saw a bus going by and I wanted to see if it was my bus. I ran out to the corner and asked this woman, who happened to be standing at the bus stop, if she was waiting for bus number thirteen.

She just nodded her head, so I said, *"oh that's good, then it has not yet passed".*

Without provocation, she started shouting, *"Oh...you people come here to use us".*

I was totally taken aback. After all, my question was about the bus. However, this lady began screaming racial slurs and calling me a bitch, saying that I did not belong here and that I should go back to my own country. I consider myself a friendly person and pride myself on never hurting anyone intentionally.

Nonetheless, I was really mad and I shot back by saying, *" use you, all I asked you was a question about the bus. Why don't you wear a sign around your neck saying don't ask me any questions!"*

She then became quite angry and started puffing herself up and approached me menacingly screaming bitch and other horrible racial insults. By this time, I could not take it anymore and I retorted by calling her a racist. I asked her if she was a native Indian, to which she answered that she was not. On that account, I told her that she did not belong here as well, and that she should go back to her own country, too! It was really ridiculous. Here two grown women screamed at each other, each one telling the other to go back to their own country! It was obvious that this woman had done this to other people before and maybe most of them just kept quiet and sank into the background. Subsequent to my shouting at her, she became quite nervous. She shrank back into her own corner, keeping very quiet and sat anxiously waiting for the bus.

The bus arrived by this time and we both got on. She sat right near the bus driver and I sat on a seat where I could still see her. I just stared at her throughout the ride giving her the dirty eye. Finally my stop came and low and behold it was her stop, too! We both got off the bus and as she crossed the street, I continued to yell at her, calling her a racist pig and telling her that it was people like her who were ruining this country! I kept on yelling, as I could not get it out of my system. I wanted to make sure that she did not do this to someone else. I did not want her to believe that she had so much authority or power over people that she could get away with this type of behavior.

However, the more interesting part was the reactions of other people I relayed my story to. My father said that I should have told her off right in the beginning. A friend of mine with a militant type of attitude told me, that I should have picked her up and thrown her across the street. While another friend, who was a physician, told me I should have been careful, as she might have been a schizophrenic. My mother questioned as to why I bother arguing with people like that. I received all these opinions and was feeling justifiably angry, as I thought I had done the right thing. In fact I thought I had walked the middle ground compared to what others told me they would have done. I really thought I had done the right thing—until about two years later.

I was at the university when I met one of the most amazing persons one could encounter in their lifetime. He was a graduate student from Ethiopia (whose name I can't recall). There was something very special about him; he had an immense inner glow and peace to him. We started speaking to each other and one day got onto the subject of racism. I told him my story, where he then proceeded to tell me his.

One day he was coming back from work around midnight, as he worked as a security guard in a factory. He was sitting in the metro and the car was empty when a skinhead got on.

The skinhead went and sat right in front of him, looked straight into my friend's eyes and said, *" I hate you niggers. You should go back to your own country!"*

Right away when I heard this, I was infuriated, hearing someone say this to such a nice guy, all in the name of his skin color. I asked my friend what did he do.

He told me that he turned to this man, looked him straight in the eye and asked him, *"why?"*

The skinhead stumbled. He did not know what to say. No one had ever asked him why, probably not even himself. The skinhead was expecting anger, violence, or fear. In contrast, he never expected someone to be so forthright as to question his beliefs.

The skin head floundered and said, *"I... I...I because you come here and steal all our jobs".*

So my friend replied calmly, *"listen my friend, I work in a factory, it is a horrible job. If you want it, I will get you a job like that any day. I am not stealing anybody's money, I work very hard and I support my family".*

To make a long story short, the conversation lasted about twenty minutes and by the end of the bus ride the skinhead turned to the student from Ethiopia and said, *" my friend, it was really nice speaking with you, and I wish you all the best".*

When he finished the story, the hair on my arms was standing. What my friend had done was take the high road and treated his enemy as a human being. My reaction had not solved anything. It did not even make me feel better. I felt terrible for screaming at this older woman. I always thought that one must fight fire with fire. However, when I saw how my friend handled his situation, I realized that he had made one less racist in the world—while I succeeded in scaring an old lady. This marked a turning point in my life.

I now view things differently. If I can take the high road, I will do it. I do not believe you can do this in all situations, especially if the guy was coming at my friend with a knife. However, if there is a possibility of doing things a better way, we then must follow it.

If our triumph only hurts another and creates further misunderstanding, then no real victory can be derived. Ultimately, if the world can be made a better place by initiating small changes into our daily life—such as the words we speak and tones with which we voice them, then as spiritual beings we are duty bound to do so.

Love & Selfless Service

"The greatness in an ideology is not, in fact, in the ideology; but it is in the subject which lives that ideology."
Swami Chinmayananda

Thought 18

To the extent one knows love— one is love. To the extent one gives, one appreciates. When one engrains gratitude in every aspect of their attitude, the result is selfless service, one of the highest forms of *Self* love.

This service can be seen in the form of a smile, compliment, blessing, or prayer. Some of the most powerful forms of currency have been penniless. It is through this currency that the flow of abundance manifests. This tide is activated through alchemy and alchemy is activated through energy.

The intention behind our thoughts are the energies in our lives. As energetic beings, living between the human mind and the cosmic mind, our thoughts lead to the purity of our service. In every action lies the intention behind the thought, and behind the intention lies the motive. Thus, by removing the motive, we clear the path to a pure intention. This leads to the purity of our service, thus producing an act that is inviolable.

In view of this, very few truly give for giving. These individuals are a rarity in life, as they work in their shadow. They have accomplished God-realization through selfless seva (service), expecting only what needs to be done. They do not keep tabs on the giving and receiving, because these thoughts are trivialities in their life.

At the end of the day, it is seva (service) that holds the greatest benefit—even though others have gained. And it is through their energy of giving, that the love of Self and God are radiated unto others, and themselves.

* * *

I can say with great conviction, that I have met only one person who fits what I have written above—he was my father-in-law, a second father and an angel in my life. His name was Madhav Rao.

Ironically, I find myself writing his story on Thanksgiving Day—the first Thanksgiving that we would find ourselves not graced by his presence. This was his holiday, where thanks emanated from and through him. I wish to share a small portion of who he was through the reflection of my eyes.

From time to time, when there is someone in our life who gives so much of himself to others, it becomes very easy to take that person for granted. My father-in-law was such a person, who gave so lovingly and yet, so altruistically.

He truly believed in anything that I did, and always unconditionally. He bestowed upon me the confidence and strength to follow the truth that lay inside of me. When I married in 1993, I wanted to open up a swimming school. It was a dream of mine to have something of my own. Many people had reservations. I had just moved to the U.S. from Canada and the notion of a small business being successful seemed like a fantasy.

I married in March and projected the school to open in September of that year. Well, it was more difficult than I bargained for. I had received over twenty rejections to rent a pool but never gave up, and neither did my father-in-law.

I recall how tirelessly he worked long-distance, helping to put together the catalog for the school. I remember when I visited him in Virginia, how he presented me with a check for $500.00 to start the school, plus the catalogs all paid and completed. He told me that it was his contribution as a father to his daughter's dream. When everyone thought it would not work, he stood by me. He was the only one who said she will do it.

The school ended up being a success within a year and exactly a year after its opening, I sold it to one of my instructors. He taught me to believe in myself, but more importantly—he embraced my visions.

He was one of the most open-minded individuals I knew. He never did unto another if he himself did not want to be treated that way. He never laughed at another if they were different or shared a view that he did not understand or agree with at that particular point in time. He listened, and through listening, would discover that what he viewed as different was actually another path of understanding. This passage of awareness was another individual's approach to life; it was the sum and substance of diversity—of humankind. This was his philosophy, his essence, and his heart.

The most remarkable aspect of my father-in-law was his heart. He gave unconditionally to anyone. This giving did not extend only to family, but especially to those who needed it whether you were a friend, an acquaintance, or a stranger. To him you were human first. The difference was that he never expected nor wanted anything back. It was never an issue, nor did it enter his mind to think in that manner.

I remember driving up to the funeral home and seeing numerous people in the parking lot waiting. I remember thinking to myself that there must be another funeral going on—but there was not. People had come from all over, each in their own way touched by his light, even if it was for only a short time.

I tried endlessly to construct words describing this wonderful *"light worker"* who incarnated for all to learn from. I had a hard time finding the exact words, until I came across a poem by Kahil Gibran. This exquisite piece of work eloquently depicts different types of givers, the last stanza characterizes my father-in-law, Madhav Rao.

> There are those who give little of the much which they have—and they give it for recognition and their hidden desire makes their gifts unwholesome.
>
> And there are those who have little and give it all.
>
> These are the believers in life and the bounty of life; their coffer is never empty.
>
> There are those who give with joy, and that joy is their reward.
>
> And there are those who give with pain, and that pain is their baptism
>
> **And there are those who give and know not pain in giving, nor do they seek joy;**
>
> **Nor give with mindfulness of virtue;**
>
> **They give as in yonder valley the myrtle breathes its fragrance into space.**

Through the hands of such as these God speaks, and from behind their eyes
He smiles upon the earth.

It is unfortunate that through one's death, only then do many of us learn to live—and that through one's death—some of us discover life's true meaning. With my father-in-law gone, I try to view the world in terms of his language, his compassion, and his spirit.

There is not a day that goes by where his thoughts do not pervade my mind. There is not a day that passes that I ponder on what he is now accomplishing behind the veil of this life. Through his passing, I have come to recognize that life inevitably lives on, but what remains constant are the memories and teachings we experience from those whom we were so blessed to know and so blessed to love.

I often find myself asking what would he do in this situation—and many times the answer lays dormant. However hard it may be for me—I try to do it, for unlike my father-in-law, I have a lot to learn about selfless love and selfless giving.

It has been a year since his passing that I write this next paragraph. And although his physical presence is no longer with us—and I cannot pick up the phone and ask him to solve my many questions as I used to—I feel his spirit inside. His essence permeates our home and has made a permanent place within my soul.

When I am in need of an answer, somehow, I know that it will be taken care of—and within hours, days or weeks, it usually is. My father-in-law gave so much to his family when he was on this plane. However, since he has left his physical body, I feel that he is doing more for his family than he ever could.

The changes that have transpired from his death have been dramatic. His essence has permeated and metamorphosed each of our spirits. I believe from where he is now, that he is helping to break down some of our fears that have been paralyzed by what we deem as 'conventional thinking'. He is furthering our development by helping us move beyond a capacity confined by boundaries, to a capacity boundless in thinking and in living. *And as we pray to our own versions of heaven—he is teaching us to capture the heaven within.*

Thought 19

Infertility is a difficult subject for anyone hoping to have a child. It becomes especially painful when you see other people start families with relative ease. All that can be said is that for reasons unknown, a universal plan is implemented where all the components fit. Life is a paradox, leaving many to wonder why some parents, who abuse or neglect their children, are graced with them so easily.

I have only this to suggest; everyone has their own karma to work out. Every soul selects the circumstances in order to work out what they feel is required for greater spiritual development from the incarnation. The same goes for abusive parents or the couple yearning for children. Each one of us must overcome, learn, and make a solid choice to deal with the cards we've chosen.

Each hardship entailed is a test that we must embrace and deal with. We enter our bodies in order to evolve our Spirit and Self. Experiences are attracted to us for the evolution of our soul. For the person who feels that they are a failure, I tell them this:

pain imparts to us that there is a problem to solve, but pain can be lessened through knowledge. As you learn to understand karma, you will learn to understand your life.

* * *

This story was told to me by a friend of mine named Michelle, who went through the process of infertility. She relates how going through the various stages brought forth a new understanding and awareness of herself, her marriage, and her life.

This is Michelle's story:

Infertility is a very difficult thing to go through—it can eat you alive if you give it permission. I know of a nurse in my workplace who kept trying for twelve years. She could never get past the point, move on and consider other options; she was stuck in a revolving cycle of treatments and ongoing expenses. To this day, she still wants to become pregnant. She becomes highly emotional upon seeing a baby or if people speak about babies.

When dealing with infertility, one needs to know when to draw the line and to seek other options. For my husband and I, we decided to seek other avenues due to financial constraints and health problems. The decision to adopt came when I had ruptured two discs in my back and had other health problems. For me it was not an easy decision to reach. I still very much wanted to continue the fertility treatments. My husband was ready to adopt much sooner than I was— years sooner.

Finally, at age 35, I went to a second infertility doctor. Here, I went through my medical history with him, informing him of my health problems and past fertility tests that were completed on me. After listening and reading all the medical history, he turned to me and said, *"What is it you expect and what is it you think that I can do for you?"*

It was at that moment that I thought— *this must be it*— I am just going to have to make a decision here and now. I can no longer go on hoping, putting both our lives on hold. I remember leaving the room and walking back to my car, the entire while realizing that I now needed to take a deep look within my Self and within my soul and ask those very questions that the doctor put to me.

This is when I took a few precious moments and thought—really thought—about my life, our life, and the direction it needed to go. An answer came from inside that guided me to a path that my husband and I were to share in. I realized that in this life, I had to accept another road to becoming a mother. I prayed and the answer came. It was always there—I just needed to unveil it.

Adoption is not for everyone and it certainly is not the final resolution to fill a void. It, however, was our path, our road to walk, and so we walked it. Together, we then made the decision to adopt.

At this printing, Michelle is the proud mother of a beautiful baby girl named Nisha. She went to India to adopt. As an addendum, nearly three years have passed since Nisha came to the U.S. and she has adapted remarkably. Her first signs of acclimatizing were when she threw her first temper tantrum in Toys 'R Us. I truly believe that unseen hands were what force drove me to be so resolutely persistent in Nisha's adoption. Despite the many unheeded warnings from the adoption agency personnel, family and well meaning friends, Nisha is a part of our lives just as if she came from me.

I can recall a sort of frantic feeling before Nisha arrived and it was not a frantic feeling from not being pregnant or from failed infertility treatments. There are those who believe that what we feel in our hearts, our souls, and our minds are what drives us to the actions in our lives. These beliefs can be born out previous lives, personal religious/ spiritual beliefs, or simply out of love. I cannot say with conviction what made me such a driven person to adopt. However, I can tell you what I do know—I love her. I feel a sense of peace for that space in my soul that seemed so restless. I have a sense that all the pieces of the puzzle are now in place. She is where she should be, here with me and I am doing what I was meant to do—be a mother and love her.

Thought 20

Become an organ donor! Our body is only a vehicle, upon death it changes into another configuration. Let someone have the opportunity to live in this plane—while your journey continues onto the next.

In this occurrence, everyone involved will encounter the seeds of love sown into the hearts of many. This selfless act furnishes birth, thus continuing the cycle in the wheel of life.

Thought 21

Adoption. I could go on about this subject, but instead I would like to share a small passage that a dear friend once told me.

I adopted my son when he was two and a half-months old. His mother was sixteen, his father seventeen, both college bound. I had always mentioned that my son was adopted ~ not as a major topic of conversation but as a matter of joyful fact.

When he was seven, I was doing dishes and he was sitting at the table.

He asked the question I knew would someday come. *"Mom, why didn't my real mother want me?"* .

I slowly turned around and said, *"Oh Chip, she did want you very much, and your father too. They loved you enough to give you what you deserved. God has two ways of getting babies to their mothers. One is growing in the stomach and that child is yours. Another way is growing in the stomach of another woman and then that baby comes to its real mother. My son grew in my heart— not in my belly."*

* * *

This is Pam Jury's story:

The idea of adopting came about when I was thirteen or fourteen years of age. I had always dreamed of becoming a mother. Around the age of fifteen I knew I had wanted the experience of being a mother, both biologically and through adoption. I grew up in the sixties, where, in that era, population explosion was a significant issue. I always wanted two children. My plan was to have one and adopt the other, as that would be my contribution in cutting back on our world population. A baby was already here on this planet that needed parents, so why have another. I always knew that there was a child out in the world that belonged to me. It was a knowing-ness inside that became so powerful one couldn't help but just know.

When I met my first husband, I told him that this is what I wanted to do. When I gave birth to my daughter, I had almost died having her and the doctors told me not to have any children for at least four to five years. This was not a problem for me, as my decision to adopt had already been made.

There was never a doubt in my mind after having my daughter, that adoption was for me. It was just a matter of the time, I was spacing my children's years, knowing they would be two and a half to three years apart. A doubt never entered my mind—*ever.*

When I look at the comparison between giving birth to my daughter and adopting my son, it is like comparing apples to oranges. There is perfection in both. They are both totally different and both totally perfect. They are complete, each one whole in their own process.

Seeing my son for the first time and being able to hold him was incredible. There was nothing like it. It was an incomprehensible experience cradling him in my arms. Many thoughts stream through your mind on how one could give such a baby up. It takes enormous strength and bravery on the part of the biological parents.

It is my belief karmically that you choose your own parents for certain lessons that you both need to learn. Well, I believe that Chip chose us as his parents. And with each birthday that passes, I always say a silent prayer to his biological parents—thanking them.

Thought 22

Forgiveness is one of the purest forms of *love*. To forgive is to overcome. To overcome is to know deep within the core of your being, that each experience which springs forth can be handled and learned from. Forgiveness goes to the very core of our inner-ness. It removes the "I and Me" within each of us.

Like an apple's core, this is our Atman (soul). Once we have learned to peel the layers and remove the substance, we are left with the seeds. It is in these seeds that forgiveness can blossom. When we forgive, we allow the Self to accept and embrace change. When one allows change to become a part of who they are, they have embraced chaos.

God loves itself and by loving ourselves we love a God who loves itself within us—this is the act of forgiveness. However, forgiving does not necessarily intend that one has to forget; it simply means remembering without bitterness.

Meditation, a Path to Empowerment

"By the practice of meditation, you will find that you are carrying within your heart a portable paradise."
Paramahansa Yogananda

Thought 23

Meditation—what is it?

There are many forms of meditation. Contemplation is one form practiced by millions unknowingly.

While you wash the dishes and find your mind astray, you are in contemplation.

While you are driving and the song takes you to another realm, you are in contemplation.

While you are in the park listening to the earth's repose and experiencing its nirvana, you are in contemplation.

While you find yourself listening to your breath and closing off all channels to sound, you have gone one step further, *meditation.*

Thought 24

The side effects of meditation…

You will find that your thinking processes become more organized as a result of meditative calmness. The body's immune system will also be strengthened and internal aging processes are slowed down. Older, long-term meditators are mentally and physically younger than their calendar years might suggest. Stress symptoms are reduced and the nervous system is refreshed and enlivened, allowing awareness to be easily infiltrated.

This all can be summed up by what a dear friend, who is an old time meditator, once told me: *"I find as a comparison, having been through therapy, I never discovered the core peace that meditation has brought me. It was subtle at first, taking about three months for me to notice its effect. But upon realizing and examining it closer, I found that this is what the Bible refers to as 'The peace that surpasses all human understanding'.*

Thought 25

Slept eight hours and still feel quite fatigued? Although sleep helps in reducing some of our tiredness, it does not aid in the years of built up anxiety self-created by us. Your body needs more than just sleep— it needs *deep rest.* What is the difference? Although we may try to eliminate stress through exercise such as walking or going to the gym, our system needs more than that.

Vacations are wonderful, but once you are back in the swing of things it does not take long to feel like you never left. Hobbies such as reading, painting, or crochet are great for reducing some stress levels, but the core can only be compassed in deep rest. This can be only initiated through some type of meditation.

Thought 26

Posture is important in meditation. Sitting upright when practicing meditation is the ideal position when possible. This pose permits the spine to stretch upward, the chest to expand and the head to be held in place with little effort. This allows for the lungs, heart, and diaphragm to work efficiently, while simultaneously maintaining its fluidity and flow.

By aligning our body in an upward and level position, we strengthen the energy of the Kuma nadi, which aids in stabilizing the base of our spine. Kurma means tortoise and nadi is the channel within our subtle body. This energy is located between the first and second chakras and helps to regulate the balance of mind and body, while the journey inward becomes realized.

Think of the Kurma nadi as the roots of a tree that sustains the trunk. It keeps the tree grounded as it develops its posture and inward process. As awareness runs up the spinal pathway of the trunk, it will integrate wholeness and initiate bloom.

However, if pain occurs due to posture, one must change the position to what feels most comfortable to them. Do not stress your body into an uncomfortable stance, as it will effect the overall meditation.

Thought 27

Meditation can be done anywhere. The only tool one needs is time. Sit in a position that feels comfortable to you. Focus on a mantra, which can be a word or sentence that is meaningful to you. One can also envision a white light or center on a particular problem. It does not matter what you focus on, as long as you feel comfortable with that image.

You could center on your children, spouse, or even a flower. Meditate on what you find captivating, for meditation is a natural part of our inner world, while concentration is not. By meditating on what appeals to you, the concentration will come. For whatever image you are focused on, it will enwrap you from inside. You will no longer feel that you are meditating, since it will facilitate a freedom of ease on its own. The image will no longer be separate from you, but constitute as an integral part of your being, an indivisible part of your reality.

The idea is to *focus* and close off from the outer world. There is no safer and loving place to be than in your Oneness. This is a place where once you become aware of its existence, no one can provoke, harm, or disrupt your equilibrium. This impenetrable and voiceless peace is the God-Mind of your soul.

Thought 28

You will find that in many South Asian homes there is a special room designated for spiritual practice and prayer. Some may call this a meditation or tranquility room, while others use it for worshiping their God. Whatever the motive, it is a place where one can go to be *with-in* and remain there undisturbed. If a room is not possible, find a region in an area of your home and appoint it as your special sanctuary where you can associate peace and serenity. Place flowers, candles or whatever you deem befitting to engage in some type of reflection that will assist in furthering your inner journey.

Since it is a room reserved for spiritual practice, those who enter are never intruded upon. Family members become accustomed to giving privacy to whoever may enter. This allows for children to become aware of spiritual practice and meditation early in their life. It aids the next generation in developing their internal existence, as they learn, grow, and prosper within the external one.

Thought 29

Sometimes just Being is fulfillment in itself. Our mind and body need time to just *Be*. When we enter into the Being mode, time is at a standstill. Our need to replenish from the Doing, encountered through daily survival, is fulfilled by simply Being. This can be applied through various modes of meditation.

Thought 30

The power of Being is the power of *living presence*. When you can take this moment and feel thankful for it—this is Being. When you wake up and end your day with a sense of gratitude for all of its summed up moments—you are living in Being.

Living in Being is a powerful place to emerge from. This is a place where nothing and everything exists simultaneously. Charisma is fostered through Being. This is what attracts many of us to a person who possesses it. They exude a sense of completion and solitude that we admire and possibly would like for ourselves.

When in Being, we come to face how small we really are. We learn that the world will continue on when we leave our bodies and that the earth is not sustained by our efforts or errors alone. As we *Be*, we come to actualize that our successes and failures are more diminutive than most of us perceive them to be. This is where the grinding process of our egos begins to fragment.

As one converges into the flowing waves of the ocean—one must dive into the moment; leaving fears, apprehensions and limitations aside. Absorption of this space must be accepted for *what it is* and for *what it is not*—this is the quintessence of Being.

Thought 31

There is beauty in silence and often when we are alone with our thoughts, it is then that we feel most receptive to God's good. It is through meditation that problems become solutions. The mental energy spent on worrying gets directed into a positive energy field, where body, mind, and spirit can embrace. The cleansing of ones inner Self, leaves the spirit boundless, yet centered.

Reflection of the Self is one of life's necessities. It helps us interpret that where chaos reigns—stability will follow. Life is not simply chaotic or stable; each is a constant of the other. When one can see serenity in chaos and chaos in serenity, one has tuned into divinity.

* * *

This story focuses on the heart and it's whisperings. In order for us hear the Divine—we must become attuned in its rhythm. This story comes from my father, Vijay Chitnis.

This is my father's story:

The year was 1974, when my wife's sister was visiting our home in Canada from India. She was to leave to go back to India in August. It was around the same time I was to fly to Iran on business. I thought it would be a good idea if my family made the trip together. We all flew to New York and then boarded Air India to its final destination, which was Bombay. After a few days I left my family with my wife's sister and I took off to Tehran, Iran, for business. Upon my return to Bombay, I was told that Air India pilots had gone on strike and that there would be no available flights until the pilots returned to work.

In the meantime, I had to return back to Tehran, Iran, because the business was unfinished. Before I left for Iran, I needed to rearrange our travel plans on another airline. Most of the other airlines were fully booked because of the strike. There was one airline that still had seats available—and that was on TWA. I walked into TWA office in Bombay and asked them if there were any seats left. They said that there was, so I booked the tickets from Bombay to New York on TWA.

Just as a matter of curiosity, I asked the agent where from Bombay to New York does the plane stop? She replied that it stopped in Rome. I was about to leave when somehow I felt that I needed to ask her one more question. I asked her if it stopped anywhere between Bombay and Rome. She said that there was a short 45-minute refueling stop in Tel-Aviv.

I was sitting on one of those swivel chairs and I turned away from her and put my head on my lap and said, *"Oh my God—no!"*

The reason for my reaction was that in those days, there used to be quite a number of hijackings and possible bombings of an aircraft from various terrorist groups. When the agent told me Tel-Aviv, it certainly frightened me. I was in two minds and was unable to make a sound decision on what to do at that minute.

The travel agent turned to me and said, *"Sir, please make up your mind. There is a long line of customers waiting."*

I turned to her in a hurry and said, *"O.K, ok fine, I'm alright, book the tickets."*

I returned home to my wife's sisters' place and told my wife that we were booked on TWA. I expressed to her that I was not comfortable with the flight path due to the air craft's stop in Tel-Aviv and its security measures.

My wife responded by saying, *"Don't be so silly, nothing like that is going to happen."*

With that comment, I tried to ignore my inner most feelings and proceeded with the rest of the vacation. We were headed to Matheran, a resort hill station in India. We returned from Matheran and I left to Iran for the second time. I went to Iran with a heaviness in my heart. I felt like I was carrying a ton of bricks on my back. I tried to console and rationalize my thoughts with what my wife had said about this being all in my mind.

Upon return, I asked my business agent Rajal Shah if there was any news on the Air India pilots returning to work.

He said, *"Oh by the way Vijay, some Air India pilots did return."*

I begged him to try to get me on one of Air India's flights, as I knew that he knew the general manager of Air India. Luckily, through Rajal we were fortunate enough to acquire all the five tickets to go back home. The night we were to return home, TWA take-off flight time was 7:00 p.m. and our flight with Air India was at 1:30 a.m. in the morning. Air India arrived late and we boarded around 2:30 p.m. that morning. Air India's stop was London and then on towards New York. When we reached London, we got off the plane, as cleaning was going to take place and then we re-boarded. Before the take-off they handed us a London newspaper. I opened the front page to see that TWA, after landing in Tel-Aviv for 45 minutes, blew up in the air over the Greek Island Corfu.

Officials concluded that a bomb was planted at Tel-Aviv.

I showed the headlines to my wife and said, *"This was the flight that we were supposed to be on".*

Back at work in Toronto I received a telex from my agent saying, *"Thank God you were not on that flight"*.

I feel that it was not our time—but more importantly I listened to my heart. That nagging, beseeching voice that simmered below all my rationalizations is what saved us. If I can pass anything on to another person from this story, it would be to give your Self some quiet time to hear that voice. I believe what made me ask the travel agent that second pertinent question, if the flight stopped anywhere between India and Rome, was because I gave heed to a feeling that came from deep inside.

I felt that something was not right—although it should have well been by the looks of the flight pattern. Usually there is only one stopover and it would have made perfect sense to stop in just one country. But at that minute I felt compelled to ask if there were any additional stopovers. I give credence to trusting my inner voice and allowing myself to go beyond reason. I have no doubt that by the grace of God this is why we are alive and well today.

Thought 32

Meditation is a necessary part of our daily life. It should be as automated as food and drink is to our daily existence. Meditation and prayer go hand in hand. Prayer is the outgoing of thoughts to whatever Supreme power you believe in, while meditation is the incoming murmurings voiceless yet received.

The channels of our inner consciousness can only be tapped through some type of inner reflection. Once these arteries are unplugged, your awareness will become more acute. As you learn to unplug from the external world and center on your internal existence, love of Self and nature will exude.

It will become harder to kill even the most minute of creatures. Why? Through meditation, inner reflection and spiritual readings, your silence will begin to internalize how interconnected we all are to each other, this planet and other planes of existence.

This is the essence of spiritualism.

Thought 33

According to Vedic science, human beings have four bodies. Each body relates to a different state of consciousness, and each encasement insulates the Atman (inner being).

The first level of existence is our gross or physical body (Sthula sharira) that one views in our waking state. This waking state of consciousness contains impressions derived directly from objects presented to the senses. It is the food and breath sheaths that make up the gross or physical body.

The second level of existence is the subtle or astral body (Sukshma sharira), in which

dreams are manifested. This is our dream state. It has the same form as the physical body, but is made up of subtle matter. In this state of dream consciousness, impressions

are not directly filled from the objects, but from the images of objects stored in the memory. This sheath is composed of breath, emotion, and intelligence.

The third level of existence is our causal body (Karana sharira). This is where deep sleep emanates from. The causal is in the form of an egg shape, and is a body that is light. In this state of dreamless sleep, the senses and the mind are quiescent. This sheath is made from intelligence and bliss.

The fourth level of existence is the body of the transcendental state (Turiya), also called The Blue Pearl. This body is the subtlest of all the bodies and can be seen in a tiny form of blue through meditation. This tiny blue ball is the mirroring of our inner Self. This is our light, our being, and our soul. This wakeful state of Being is neither cognitive or non-cognitive—it rills pure awareness. It is within the Blue Pearl that the different planes of existence are contained. This is our Supracausal state of Being.

Thought 34

Listening to our inner voice—the Atman (inner divinity) can be attained through the quieting of our inner thoughts. Once a day, we should quiet our minds and listen to its whisper. This can only be done through reflection, breathing, visualization, contemplation, or meditation.

The best time to quiet the mind is the first waking hour of the morning. This is when the mind is fresh and unfettered from chaos that the day may bring. If morning is not possible, find sometime each day to be alone, even if it is for just a few minutes. Remember, since birth our minds have always been engaged in some activity—by the simple act of thinking. Repose is a necessity.

Yoga: Union of Individual Consciousness and Universal Consciousness

"I had hoped to get instructions in Yoga, expected wonderful teachings, but what the teacher did was mainly force me to face the darkness within myself, and it almost killed me."
Irina Tweedie

Thought 35

Concentration: nothing can be accomplished without it. Turning the mind *with-in* leads us to Self-mastery. The Greeks applied concentration through outward expression; the result was that great works evolved from literature and art. The Hindus concentrated on the internal expression of the Self, the result being the birth of Yoga.

Yoga is Self-conquest (actualization of the Divine Self). The benefit of Yoga is to train our mind to go beyond the relative knowledge of the senses. Through this we remove layer upon layer of our internal membrane to realize our God-Self. Yoga is a science for the liberation of the mind.

Through concentration of the mind on studying itself, one reaches ones own belief, own reality, and own eternity. The goal of Yoga is to unearth the innermost recesses of your mind and then to form your own conclusion.

Since Divinity is Universal, no faith or religious belief system is necessary in Yoga. Believing in what you have found through your own mind-mastery is the essence of Yoga and the sum and substance of freedom. It is only through meditation that we can unlock the gates of nature and let the light inward—flow outward.

* * *

This story comes from a Hatha Yoga instructor named Dorothy. Her story may not be one that is earth-shattering or dramatic, but is one that connotes *pure simplicity*. It comprises the little things in her life that provide her with freedom of living and freedom of life. Whether it is physical, mental, or spiritual, Dorothy has unveiled contentment through life's intricate subtleties. This is what Dorothy has to say on union, life, and yoga:

This is Dorothy's story:

I was out shoveling snow and the snow blower broke down. Consequently, I picked up a shovel and I started shoveling the driveway, thinking nothing of it. I said hello to my neighbor and finished a few hours later. The next day, my neighbor came up to me and asked me how I was feeling.

I said, *"fine, why do you ask"?* The neighbor replied, *"you were out there shoveling for hours, you have a very long driveway and it took you all afternoon. Are you sore at all? How can you walk"?*

I was not sore, nor was I tired. It did not even occur to me that this would be anything out of the ordinary, yet my neighbor made me aware that most people would find this exhausting. However, to me, I did not even think about shoveling the driveway by hand. *This is freedom.* I was able to do something and not think about how I might feel the following day.

Tying my shoes is another example of freedom. How many people need to sit down on a chair and tie their shoes? I do not think about it. I do not contemplate the repercussions, as yoga summons physical and mental strength within me. *This is liberation.* It is deep, powerful, and yet uncomplicated.

Another aspect that yoga brings forth is my internal reaction. Anything that I may encounter as chaotic or unsettling, I take a deep breath. If someone is angry with me or if I am angry with them, *I breathe.* I do it automatically without thinking. It is not to say that I am less angry or that things go anymore smoothly. It, however, provides me with the ability to stop and quiet my mind. This allows me to take notice of what is really happening, not what my emotions perceive is happening.

This rationale stems from my yoga practice. My automatic response is not to react to my feelings. This does not mean that I do not have any feelings. What it means is that I can step back from where I am in that minute and observe the situation from a different perspective. It warrants me to be a little calmer and slightly more balanced. *Now, how many people go through life with that reaction?*

Retaining the liberation to believe in something deeper than what I am, is done by taking one breath— in that second. It does not mean that circumstances might change. Life still goes on, yet I am able to go *within* for just a moment. This allows me to have freedom from reaction and view reality as it is. Here, I truly react to the present moment, as I am not concerned for the past, nor afraid of the future. This grants me deliverance from mind and body, resulting in ease of living in present time. It is in these small things that a big difference is brought about.

Yoga takes care of my body, mind, and spirit. Within the quietude of yoga, my Authentic Self is made visible. Once the mind is free from the roles we play, only then can the soul emerge. Thus begins the quest for me to reach out for something deeper, such as why am I here? What is it that I can contribute to this world, and how can I make another person's life easier? This is my spiritual Self, but this becomes very hard to do when the body is aching and the mind is troubled. Thus, this is the freedom that yoga produces.

I do not live from story to story, from tragedy to tragedy or from joy to joy: yoga signifies the 'in between'. It captures the small stuff. Sometimes many of us tend to look for the big events such as getting married, having a child, retirement, etc. But what happens to all the bits in between, all the days, hours, and seconds? This is the core of yoga. This is what makes yoga alive, when we are living not from event to event, but from moment to moment.

Thought 36

Yoga and meditation are not only for adults, but should be introduced to a younger age group. This is a powerful way of building a child's esteem. To enable them to perceive and discern internally will strengthen their ability to react appropriately externally in their childhood years. The application of these skills will strengthen and empower their sense of Self, granting them to behold stability within the chaos. The harmonizing of these two opposites into one finite scope will harvest *balance*.

We must think of our life in terms of an inner circle spiraling outward from within other circles. The outermost comprises humanity, while the inner circles represent society, community, and family.

Everything must begin at the core of this circle and work its way out. This innermost core represents who we are. It does not matter in which culture or religion you are raised or whether you live in the Western or Eastern part of the world. Fallacies begin when one believes that their culture is superior or the only way of living life; this is what Hindus label maya (illusion). We seem more caught up in living in duality and separateness. This type of thinking is seen not only in the West but is rampant in the East as well.

Unfortunately, there is a great misconception that culture and environment raise good children. If we are unable to see that we must begin at the apex of the triangle and then work downwards, we will continually find ourselves in a revolving door, wondering which passage is the correct one. For culture and environment nurture only a portion of the whole. The majority comes from a reality beyond the five senses. This reality is intangible. Once this light is lit within—only then can its flare spread to family, community, society, and eventually humanity.

However, this light must begin with us individually and must end with us collectively in order to break down the spheres of separation and duality.

* * *

I have been graced with the opportunity of having seen a small portion of the world at a relatively young age. Due to this, I have been able to observe and understand how some cultures experience and embrace life. I have come to discern how minute our perspectives on life can occasionally be. When we think ethnocentrically about the culture in which we live, we leave ourselves open to ignorance, and ignorance causes us to think narrowly about who we are. I have viewed this type of thinking from both sides of the world, East and West.

I believe that ignorance is manufactured to a degree equal to ones own fears. The dominant foundation of ignorance is fear of the unknown and fear of change. In conversations when one is uncertain of something, one is usually apprehensive of the change it might bring to their lives and to the lives of their family. Change is eminent—if we are to live in this plane of existence.

The construct of the inner circle working its way outward is reversed when ignorance is involved. Conversely, the outer circles are working their way inward, resulting in the surroundings affecting the individual, family, community etc. The inner core of the circle must remain firmly established in order for the outer circles to be affected in a positive manner. Consequently, whether you live in India, England, or Iceland will be of little significance if the inner core of who you are is absent of substance.

By knowing the world within greater than living in the world without—we become more apt to seeing other cultures not as good, bad or separate—but as another part of life we have yet to experience, learn and appreciate.

Thought 37

While the West began studying Consciousness in the nineteenth century, Consciousness has been part of East Indian religion and philosophy for nearly 3000 years. A part of this has been incorporated into the language of the chakras.

The chakras are a vital part of Eastern teaching. They are the activity centers through which our spiritual and emotional energies flow. The word chakra is Sanskrit and means *wheel of energy*.

The spine is pictured as a tree, where seven centers or chakras are located at specific points on the spine. These centers are assembled into a vertical structure from the tailbone to the crown of the head. The spiritual energy on the spine is imaged as a feminine serpent. The name of the serpent is called the Kundalini (the coiled up one). It is thought of as being coiled up at the base of the spine. This motion of being coiled is seen as an immense reserve of spiritual energy. When this energy is aroused, it unweaves and elevates up the spine through these seven centers of Consciousness. As the Kundalini awakens, it alters and transforms our Consciousness, the Being within, to produce varying degrees of enlightenment.

The chakras are not a system which can be viewed by the untrained eye. This is why Western medicine (although acquiring a better understanding) often does not understand the yogic systems which incorporates the Kundalini and the chakra systems as a necessary part of reaching a harmonic balance.

The goal of yoga and meditation is to bring this serpent power up the spine to the head in order that our entire being brings forth balance and healing. The correct flow of spiritual energies through the chakras is necessary for a balanced mind, body, and spirit. A blockage in the current of energy can produce a variety of dysfunction, some of which are: feeling of disease, lack of balance, highly sensitive, intellectual arrogance, manipulation of words—verbal abuse, attachment to material possessions, physical wants and high ego needs.

The nervous system is similar to the Kundalini system, as one will find a chakra location usually near nerves that are bundled tightly together. Chakras are balls of energy within our physical bodies that permeate through two major vehicles; the endocrine glands and a group of nerves called the plexus. Each chakra is associated with one of the seven endocrine glands and the plexus. Vibrating at a certain frequency, these elements become subtler as they move up the scale. Moving through the five physical elements of earth, water, fire, air, and ether, to the spiritual elements of inner sound and inner light. The heaviest element rests on the bottom, while the lightest remains on top.

·The first chakra is located at the base of the spine and is called Muladhara. Mula means root and Adhara means support. This chakra is associated with the earth and its sense is smell. The basic principle that this chakra emulates is acceptance and contact with the energy of this planet. If this chakra is open, one will have a deep sense of Oneness to themselves, others, and the planet. This connection will bring forth stability, contentment and inner strength. This chakra gives us our sense of 'grounding' and forms our foundation. We will flow with our physical existence and blend with the harmonic energy that is pervasive on this plane. Shaping our existence through prana (life force) thereby reaching our life goals effortlessly.

·The second chakra is called Svahisthana and is located just above the genitals. Sva means that which is itself and histhana means its actual place. This chakra is associated with water and its sense is taste. It is through this chakra that a person feels their deepest feelings. Svahisthana allows for the body to communicate to the Being inside, to its needs and wants. When this chakra is opened, grace, depth of feeling, sexual fulfillment, and ones ability to be adaptable is brought forth. Harmonious functioning of this chakra develops open and trusted flow of our interpersonal relationships. The union of male and female energies within us allows for intimacy that is all-embracing, thus augmenting a totality of completion in sexual union.

·The third chakra is called Manipura and is located at the solar plexus. Manipura means city of jewels. This chakra is associated with fire and its sense is sight. When this chakra is opened, a person can achieve sereneness and remain undisturbed in stressful situations. Acceptance of oneself in all situations is at work when the third chakra is opened. As wisdom and abundance perforates the wall of intellectual understanding, one will work in automatic harmony through life's ups and downs. This chakra plays a role in ones connectedness to the world around them, and how one view's power, control, and freedom.

·The fourth chakra is called Anahata and is located at the eight vertebrae of the spine opposite of the heart. Anahata means unbeater. This chakra is associated with air and its sense is touch. The heart chakra is a source of which light and love emulate in divine and human form. When this chakra is sentient, a person's intuition increases and they are more attuned to their surroundings both on the physical and astral planes. The heart chakra allows us to love deeply, thus radiating our energies unto the auras of others. When this same energy is extended outward, we have the capacity to heal and dissipate negative vibrations in others. It gives us the faculty to envelop a true empathetic nature toward other individuals. One will acquire a greater understanding that, in order to achieve perfect union of who we each are, we must embrace separation. In doing so, we will incorporate a more involved sense of tranquility and Self-centeredness.

·The fifth chakra is called Visuddha and is located from the base of the neck near the third cervical vertebra. Visuddha means pure. This chakra is associated with the element of ether and its sense is hearing. Visuddha encircles the aspects of expressing and receiving; it is the basic law of Universal abundance, where ones desires and needs are always taken care of when surrendering into the hands of divine power. When Visuddha is opened, awareness is multiplied in our mental body and we are no longer dominated by the physical and emotional senses—our objectivity becomes acute. We have a keen sense that we co-exist on other planes of life; one being—our inner dimension. It is here that the Higher Self guides us, forming an unwavering certainty of knowing. This knowing leads us to the path that we are to partake in, in this lifetime. As this chakra awakens, we become cognizant of these subtler planes of Being and in doing so, we allow it to infiltrate and absorb our Consciousness. The knowledge received from these subtler spheres of Being are conveyed to others when the time is most opportune. This imparts in us the confidence to remain steadfast in who we are and what we say, instead of becoming easily swayed. It opens the passageway to silence and listening, while clarity of communication heightens. We will notice that although one may not agree or understand what we voice, the clarity and flow of our language will leave seeds that may one day be sown.

·The sixth chakra is called Ajna and is located between the eyebrows. This is known as the third eye or eye of wisdom. Ajna means command. This chakra is associated with the element of inner sound, a communication that is of the internal sense, not dependent on the physical world. It is seen by Eastern traditions as a necessary step to spiritual growth and enlightenment. Its sense is all senses, including extrasensory perception. This is the chakra that seats our mental sphere of Being. Persons with this chakra in harmonious function tend to have a level head yet at the same time are open to the mystical truths. When this chakra is open, one's perception and awareness is expanded beyond the five physical senses. Deep and abstract tenets are recognized and are expressed. The third eye is also associated with our extra sensory perception (ESP). When awakened, one will experience images or visions within one's Consciousness ephemerally, allowing perception and intuition to arise effortlessly. A strong sixth sense, clairvoyance, and an insight to other dimensions beyond the physical are evident. The third eye is the place of vision where one can see the past, present, and future. It is through this eye of wisdom that the process of physical sight is not necessary in order to see. As this eye expands, one will view images as clearly as one does through physical sight. It is here that one starts to experience the Blue Pearl and its different realms of existence. Healing through mental projection also blossoms. It is within this chakra that a person experiences their *Oneness* and completion of Self.

·The seventh chakra is called Sahasrana and is located at the crown of the head or can be found hovering slightly above the head. Sahasrana means a thousand-petaled lotus. It glows in all colors, but the dominant color is violet. This chakra is associated with the element of inner light or white light and this is the most subtle of all elements, metaphysically speaking. It is here where one delves into the abysmal core of their Being. It is within this chakra that our cosmic consciousness lies, the *I Am* center. When this chakra is opened and cognizant, one will find oneself in a world where neither time nor space exist. This is the place of *'all knowing'*. It is here where one can experience a sense of being out of one's body, in states of meditation. As this chakra opens, we will no longer feel division or become separated by our perceptions. Rather, we will come to know how birth-less and death-less we really are—and then we will come to acknowledge that we are truly Beyond.

Thought 38

Attention to detail can sometimes be lost by the very achievement of its goal. Paying attention to the substance and its minute parts is where great success emanates from. But many of us are caught up with the end results, rarely paying care to the means. By giving proper attention to the means through strengthening, enhancing, and caring, only then can the end follow. Success starts by paying as much attention to the means as you do the ends. Failure arises when the means are neglected. For it is the cause that produces the effect. With a weak cause there can be no effect.

Remember, when something is perceived as powerful, it really has no strength, and when something is viewed as powerless, that is where the strength lies.

Divine Intervention

"That which cannot be comprehended by the mind,
but by which the mind comprehends;
that which encompasses the mind-
know that to be Brahman.
That which cannot be seen by the eyes,
But by which the eyes see-
Know that to be Brahman."

Kena Upanishad

Thought 39

Answers to your questions are everywhere! In the next movie you might view, in a line you read from a book or from a few words verbalized by a friend. We are constantly being shown—only some signs may not be quite as obvious as others.

Guidance is given continually to us from unseen hands; however, many of us are not sensitized enough to perceive them. This is partly due to fear of the unknown and focusing on a world where the externals outweigh the internals.

We are a race that cannot get enough information and yet, we are a race starved for a knowledge greater than that of who we are. However, when we do receive signs, many of us either reject or deny their existence. This is the paradox that we often find ourselves caught up in. We search, find, deny or reject, and than we continue seeking.

We must take notice *now* and accept these daily hints as not innocuous figments, but of a path assisted by whatever Power or God we give credence to.

* * *

This story comes from a lady whom I will call Betsy. Betsy is self-employed in the area of house cleaning, which is how we became acquainted. She has become a dear friend and always lightens up my home with her candid spirit. To me, Betsy is an old soul, and I feel privileged to recount her experience.

This is Betsy's story:

The year was 1970. I had just given birth to my youngest daughter, Selia. I was experiencing pain in the abdomen region and could not figure out what it was. I went to see the doctor who then had ordered some tests to be done. When the tests came back they said that I had gallstones. Alongside having the gallstones, I was also experiencing appendicitis attacks. It was hard to distinguish which was which. At that point my physician did not even know that it was appendicitis. I was scheduled to have surgery.

I was in the prep room getting ready for surgery when I had another unknown appendicitis attack. In surgery, the doctors would soon realize that my appendix had ruptured. As they wheeled me to the elevator, I remember looking at my husband Doug and being overwhelmed by this feeling that I may not come out of this. I remember telling Doug that I did not want to go, I just did not want to have this surgery done. I kept feeling that I would not see my three children again.

The next thing I remember is that I was hovering above my body. I remember looking down at myself and watching the physicians frantically try to revive my heart. I could see them looking over at me while I was looking over them watching myself. I kept seeing myself being pulled apart by the doctors but not feeling anything. I felt as weightless as a feather and did not feel any type of emotional or physical pain. The peace that was permeating inside of me was fear-free. It is a very difficult concept to explain, but it felt that there was nothing to be afraid of anymore. All of these new types of emotions were taking place as I hovered over my body.

Then the room lit up with immense brightness. A few moments later I was looking at a long hall that had no walls—it was not a tunnel but a wall-less passageway that had a rail light at the end of it. As I felt myself moving up closer and closer to this luminous and translucent light, it began to become bigger and brighter. This feeling of peace kept intensifying as I was entering its domain. I remember hearing voices similar to people chatting—however, I cannot recall what was being said. The voices were coming from around the light. And then all of a sudden everything just stopped—I did not proceed any further.

Then I saw an outline of a man's face— it was not very clear as it was more of a silhouette form, but it was definitely a face of a male figure.

He said to me, *"don't be afraid—it is not your time"*.

This voice was so comforting and yet very powerful. I thought that this voice and the silhouette form was God. Again, I go back to this peaceful feeling, because that was what was emanating from this light. I felt like one body with this light and silhouette. It was like the melding of my heart and my soul into His. It felt like one body, one heart, and one soul.

Here, I was so panicky and worried about so many things going into surgery and then when I was in this light I found myself not wanting to ever leave its presence. A few moments passed when I felt myself being driven back—facing the light, but going further and further away. There are just no words to explain the various emotions I received. One would really have to get into my mind to see what I witnessed and felt.

I do not remember entering my body. All I remember is coming out of sedation. I had been heavily sedated for several days and was finally coming to. The minute I awoke I had remembered what had happened to me.

My husband came to my side and said, *"you know that your heart had stopped"*.

My physician came to see me.

He patted my hand and said, *"we almost lost you—your heart had stopped. You were worse than what we had originally thought"*.

He told me then that my appendix had ruptured while having the stones removed. He said that I was having appendicitis attacks at the same time my gall bladder pain was occurring.

I said, *"I know."*

However, I did not tell him what had occurred. I did not say anything to anyone until I went home. I then relayed my story to my husband to gauge a reaction. I told him what I had experienced with the light and the vision and told him that I found myself floating over my own body. He looked at me as if I had been hallucinating. From then on, I did not say too much to others. This became a personal thing that

I knew to be the truth—but it remained inside. I knew what happened and I knew what I had seen, felt and heard.

Since that experience I became closer to God. It gave me a knowing-ness inside of myself that I never had before. It gave me the strength to leave my husband, who was a wife beater. He would come home from work after running around on me and beat me because he felt guilty. I would usually get hit about three to four times a week, which usually meant he was with another woman at those times.

My husband, who was in the police force at that time, was a regular drug user. He fathered a child with one of the women he saw. It was a lot to take and one day I said no more. After this experience something inside of me was telling me that I had had enough. I told Doug that I was going to leave him and he said that we really needed to try because of the kids. At that moment I thought well, maybe he was right—but I had this uneasy feeling inside that things were not going to change and that I needed to get out with the children, as they did not need to grow up with this violence at home. The kids at that time were very young. Lauren was six, John was four, and Selia was about five months.

However, I gave it another shot with the hope that it might change. I stayed in the marriage a little less than four years. I really wanted to believe in him. The incident that finally shook me to my senses came when I was home reading one of my Bible story books. Doug came in, saw what I was reading and became very upset with me. He took the book from my hand, threw it on the floor and then proceeded to beat me.

About a week later he had his uniform on and he told me that he was scheduled to work the night shift. So, I called up the police station to see if he was indeed working. They told me that he was off. I was so angry.

My daughter Lauren who must have been close to ten at that time came to me and said, *"Mom, I will help you"*.

We threw all his clothes out on the lawn. I was not proud that my daughter had to help trash her father's clothes. I know it was wrong—kids should never be involved, but it happened. He came home early the next morning and was pounding on the door. I just stood in the doorway, not wanting to unlock it. I knew that if he got inside, he more or less would have done some serious damage or killed me in the process of trying to.

From the door I said, *"go and to stay at one of your girlfriends. Collect your clothes and get out!*

He then said, *"I am going to get an attorney and sue you for ruining my clothes!"*

It had rained that night and his clothes were all wet. My daughter was laughing in the background as she heard her father ranting and raving about his clothes. That was all he cared about; he could care less for the kids or our well being. His only concern was what would the neighbors think seeing him pick his clothes up from the lawn. I went to see an attorney and started the proceedings for a divorce.

Doug had called me and said, *"just make sure that I am not served at work, you can do it anywhere else but work"*.

I then proceeded to try to make a life for our three children and myself. I sold my wedding rings to buy a car. For the $1,500.00 set they gave me $300.00 and with that I purchased an old Chevrolet. We then had to look for another place. His parents owned the house and we were paying them by land contract. His parents gave me thirty days to vacate.

This is how strongly I feel that God's presence has been with me throughout everything I have done. One day I remember staying up late, praying and thinking where would we find shelter next and how would I have enough money to feed my children. On the last day that I was to live there a house became available for rent suddenly. I also received the exact amount of money from my work and a little from my father to help pay for the first and last months rent. It seemed that every time I prayed and asked, there wasn't anything that the kids and I went without.

I remember one incident where I had an electric bill over $100.00 and I was earning $3.35 per hour, which was minimum wage at that time. Those were difficult days, as I had three kids to support as well. That night I prayed and asked for guidance. Our electricity was to be shut off in two days and I did not have a penny to put forth. The next day I went to pick up my mail and within a bunch of bills was a check from my income tax return. This amount covered the electric bill and many other accounts that were piling up. I ended up paying all my bills and even had a little extra. I decided to celebrate with the kids by taking them to McDonalds, which in those days was a rarity. They were so thrilled. They thought that was the best celebration ever! The divine thing about this is that I had just filed my tax forms and was not expecting to receive anything for another six to nine weeks!

That same year Christmas was looking bleak. I did not have any money to buy the children Christmas presents. I just had enough to pay the bills, buy food and purchase enough gas to get me to work. The kids wanted this video game called Atari. It was quite popular at that time and it was also very expensive to buy, about $125.00. Well, my mother and my stepfather were at McDonalds one day. He had one of those scratch off tickets where different types of prizes were being given away daily. He scratched off his ticket to find that he had won an Atari video game. Needless to say, the children had something under the tree and it was something that the three of them loved and wanted. I remember wrapping it up and placing that one gift under the tree. When they awoke Christmas morning and opened it—they went crazy—they were screaming with delight. They hugged and kissed me, saying that that was the best present they had ever received!

Whatever occurred that day in surgery has changed my entire perspective on how I view who I am and the choices I make. It gave me the strength to get out of an abusive marriage and have the reliance that God will take care of my children and me. I am no longer afraid of death. I now recognize that there is another plane of existence. I can feel it and know that it is not as far as some of us may perceive it to be. The way I think of life today is that we are all at a way station. Some people get on, as their time of completion has arrived, while others get off, to learn and experience the lessons that this existence offers.

I now believe that there are many people who sleepwalk through life, looking at the world with eyes that are sealed. They seem not to be aware—they tend to go through the motions—like a robot. I may not be all there—but I think I am into the first stages of awakenment and that is having the ability to be aware. Part of having awareness is learning not to discount things just because you may not agree nor have had a similar experience.

I have become very open to different types of truths. I believe that everybody has his or her own vision of God. But the difference for me lies in my perception. You can be Catholic, Buddhist, Moslem, Jewish or whatever— but in my eyes all paths lead to the same Being. If there were only one path— there would not be so many scriptures and truths for humans to find solace in.

Today, I view all sides of a coin and retain an open attitude. I have found that it takes more energy to be ignorant—the barriers of fear and insecurity are always at your disposal when one is unaware. It is when one can journey beyond that initial step does one develop a higher sensitivity for their surroundings and Self. Thus, fracturing the walls of narrow-mindedness and arrogance as the seal that has kept the eyes fastened—begins to unglue. And I tell you—what a liberating feeling that is…

Thought 40

Nothing happens by chance. There are no coincidences. All pieces eventually fit, as synchronicity is in motion. Incidents, timing and karma play a role in bringing events together. This does not mean we can relax, sit back and let destiny do its job. What this suggests, however, is that inevitably we all find *our calling*. We need only develop our internal existence to recognize this.

If you see the world through the mask of the five senses you might find a world without cause and justice. On the other hand, if you view the world through the lens of spiritual eyes, you will recognize hidden clues that lay within each coating.

Hence, what we label as coincidences or unusual events, are really traces that hold the answers to our search. Dreams that materialize or awaken us with a strong sense, chance encounters, gut feelings or a knowing-ness that constitutes complete certainty, whereupon information is revealed without understanding how you arrived at it, are just some of the numerous signs that Spirit provides for us.

Soon, what may seem as chance or luck is actually where one must be at a particular time and place. It is what some may refer to as *perfect timing.*

* * *

This story comes from a woman named Kate, whom I had the pleasure of getting to know at one of the local businesses where she works. This story symbolizes the unique existence of extrasensory perception versus what we deem in our dimension as reality. All names have been disguised for privacy protection.

This is Kate's story:

The year was 1997 when my mother went to visit my brother in Oregon. On her return home she was told that she had mitro valve problems. She went to her physician, who strongly recommended surgery immediately. Her surgery was scheduled a few weeks later. After the surgery was completed my mother was still not recovering, so she called the hospital to make an appointment with the physician who operated on her. She was told that she was dismissed from his care and that what she was experiencing is part of the recovery process.

Months went by and she was still not getting any better. She could barely move from the bed to the chair. I told my father that he needed to take some action, call somebody or write a scathing letter to the hospital, which he then did. He wrote to the hospital saying that his wife was dying and that somebody needed to do something. The hospital readmitted her and found that her mitro valve was leaking, which was the same problem she went into the hospital to have repaired. Apparently during surgery, the physician had replaced the wrong valve and instead changed the aortic. My father and mother were speechless. My mother said that she felt as though she had been struck down by lightening. This mishap led to thrombosis forming on her mitro valve. A decision was made to go in and have it done again. This was not supposed to be a major operation. It was a routine procedure, however, her heart had weakened in the months after her first surgery due to it working so hard.

The week before my mother was to go into surgery, I was awakened at 4:00 a.m. by a feathery brush up against my neck. The feeling that I awoke with was that my mother had come to say good-bye to me. It was so real that I knew exactly what it was and why it was happening. I went back to sleep and at 8:00 a.m. I called my mother and told her that I was awoken early in the morning with a strong impression that she had died.

She said, *"No Kate, I am still around"*.

I knew this feeling was unusual as it overwhelmed my senses. Death was not on my mind as we were assured that this was standard procedure. The doctor told us that she would have a good extended life after this operation.

When she finally did go in to be prepped for surgery, my father kissed her and the anesthesiologist turned to her and said, *"Rosemary, what are you going to dream about"?*

My mother turned to him and said, *"heaven"*.

Surgery went well. Everything flowed smoothly until the end, when they could not get her heart to start beating on its own. I was in Oregon with my brother at that time and we were hiking up a mountain. This particular day was real misty and serene. When we reached the top of the mountain there were trails of wild flowers that lined a downward path, and the atmosphere was surreal. It was here that I had an eerie feeling that something was wrong.

I turned to my brother Frank, and said, *"why don't we call the hospital and see how she is doing. I don't know, but I have a bad feeling about this. I do not feel comfortable, something is not quite right"*.

We came home and called the hospital. We found out that my mother was in critical condition. They could not get her heart beating on its own but were still working on her. So my brother and I waited by the phone to hear any word that may come.

My little niece in the meantime came to my brother and I and said, *"Oma is dead, but that is O.K. I am not crying— and you should not cry either"*.

Within minutes we received a phone call saying that my mother had passed away. The bizarre thing about this is that my niece was not with us when we phoned the hospital nor was she aware of her grandmother's critical condition.

The day my mother died, the chaplain in the hospital told us that there was a little girl who was also struggling to live. This baby was an orphan, as the mother, a mentally challenged woman, was raped at a home where she resided. The baby had just undergone heart surgery and was in ICU. A glass wall was all that separated the baby from my mother. The medical staff were working on my mother and the baby simultaneously when both hearts stopped at 9:00 p.m. Everyone present that night cried. They felt that my mother was taking care of this orphan baby as they both went on to the next stage of life.

The morning after she died it was real misty and rainy.

My brother turned to me and said, *"look at the sky, even the heavens are crying"*.

The night of her death I went to sleep in her bed in Oregon and this is where she came to me in a dream. She was driving a car and I saw her grayish white hair as I sat behind her.

She said, *"Kate, now you can see me, but pretty soon you will only be able to feel me"*.

She was right—*I feel her.* They say that when somebody dies you are left with a void, you feel an emptiness beyond comprehension, but I didn't, because she told me that I wouldn't. She told me that she would always be with me, and she really is. I mean I can *feel* her—I can actually *feel* her.

We took her ashes back to Oregon. This was where my mother was going to live the remaining years, here up in the mountains on my brother's farm. At my brother's ranch, he opened the gates and let all the goats, horses and dogs follow us up the mountain. My brother has a pony for his daughter. My niece rode the pony while the rest of us followed our dad, as he held the urn in his arms and walked up the mountain to bury his wife.

My mother's death has given me a strength that I never dreamt I could have. I see things more realistically now. I do things that I would have never done before. I took her place when my father was ill, which entailed that I had to be what she was. This made me grow up much faster. I was finally able to obtain a divorce which I was afraid to do for twenty years. I should have never been with this man in the first place as he was abusive both mentally and physically to me. This was something that my mother had always hoped I could do for the sake of my own well-being. The week of Mother's Day, I filed for divorce. It was a gift to myself and a gift to her.

I do not live to fear life. I deal with life differently since her death. Falling apart at the slightest crisis was something that came to me easily. Now I just handle each moment as it carries me. Her death did not scare me as I thought it would. I really thought I would feel deserted and empty. Ironically, my heart is full, brimming more with security and love ever than before. For now, I feel that there are two of us instead of one.

I feel my mother's spirit in and around me. She is the one constant that remains a part of who I am. I have come to understand through the message she imparted to me, that she is gone for only a short period of time. Nothing is final. There is no finality to life, just a temporary physical separation. When my time is done here on Earth, and the lessons I have learnt are completed, we will be reunited—but for now I take comfort in knowing that a part of her is nestled somewhere deep inside my very breath, somewhere between my heart and my soul.

Thought 41

Divine beings are among us. Since the beginning of time we have acknowledged them and they before time have acknowledged us. Divinity is omnipresent—it can be seen in the touch of a friend, or in a smile that a stranger sends, where eyes meet for just a fleeting moment—we are never alone.

The Universe has provided us with company; through physical and non-physical means. Whether we choose to recognize them depends on our level of awareness and how attuned we are to their particular level of frequency.

* * *

This story comes from Gillian. I met Gillian through my husband and soon realized what an old soul she is. Gillian shared this story with me.

This is Gillian's story:

Growing up in England, I had an aunt to whom I was very close. My aunt and my grandmother had a very close relationship. They lived near each other in a small town in England. In October 1972, my grandfather died of liver cancer. His death happened soon after he had told the family. My grandfather was a stoic man, a philosopher by nature and a man who loved my grandmother dearly. His biggest concern before he passed on was his wife and her well-being. When he passed on, my grandmother starved herself to death and slowly began to lose all sense of reality. Aunt Doreen was going back and forth from her house trying to take care of her mother who really just wanted to die.

One day as my aunt was trying to comfort her mother by telling her that things will get better, my grandmother turned around to her and said, *"not to worry Doreen, you will follow me soon after"*.

Aunt Doreen thought to herself what a strange thing to say. At first she thought that her mother wanted her to follow her somewhere. It did not enter any of our minds that my grandmother would die soon after— about three months later. My grandmother died of a broken heart. We were all devastated. Aunt Doreen was trying to cope with losing both her mother and father within a three-month period and also prepare for her son's wedding in October. My own mother had gone to America, so my children and I spent a lot of time with my aunt Doreen.

My aunt started to become sick. The first sign was that her nails became discolored. She was one of those women who always took care about her appearance. She was always well groomed. She was showing me her nails and asking what I thought it could be as I was a nurse. The doctors thought that it was some type of fungus and really did not know where it originated. It was during that time that my aunt received her first dream of her mother. She dreamt that her mother was in this beautiful field. The field was a green meadow filled with daisies. Her mother was a long way off in the meadow motioning for her to come and join her. Her mother was beckoning her with her hands for her to come to where she was standing in the meadow. My aunt told me about this dream and said that it had bothered her as my grandmother said to my aunt that she would follow her soon.

I said to my aunt jokingly, *" don't worry about it, you are just hallucinating due to the toxicity from your nails!"*

About three weeks later she became sick again with a terrible rash all over her body. When I saw her, she asked me if this looked liked the measles. I told her that it looked similar to poison ivy. However, bells were now going off in my head thinking back to the toxicity in her nails and now the rash. The doctors could not pinpoint what the rash was either. The rash lasted about two weeks before it disappeared. It was at that time that she received her second dream from her mother. It was the same meadow with the same daisies; the only exception to the dream was that her mother was closer. My grandmother was much closer compared to the first dream, and again she was beckoning with her hands for my aunt to follow her. In both the dreams my aunt told me that my grandmother looked very lovely and happy.

My aunt's health was ok for a while, however, she began to get more symptoms that seemed unrelated to each other such as chest pains and terrible indigestion. The doctors thought that she might have some type of tumor inside of her. They decided to do an exploratory laparoscopy, where they opened her up. When they were able to look inside they found cancer everywhere, it was in her liver, pancreas and beyond. They could do nothing but close her up again; it was too late for any type of treatment. The physicians gave her six weeks to live.

My aunt returned home after her surgery. I would come and visit with her every day after work. We would sit and chat, sometimes I brought my children with me and she always made sure there was some type of sweets or biscuits for them. Towards the last few weeks of her life, her health deteriorated rather quickly and that was when she received her third and final dream from her mother. This time her mother was at the edge of the pastoral meadow holding her hand out for my aunt to place her hand in my grandmother's. She said that this time she could feel her hand in her mother's hand, and she knew that this time she was going to the other side. She had this dream two nights before she passed away. She relayed the last dream to me the night before she died—and she told me that she was going to the meadow where her mother would be waiting for her. The next morning she was unconscious and that evening she passed on—October 1973.

It was a few months later, sometime in January on a Saturday afternoon, when I was driving on a main road to my in-laws with my two children in the back seat. Altogether it was a miserable day, as the rain poured down heavily. We were driving along when all of a sudden I started to smell this perfume in the car. The scent started out faint, but I also felt a presence—as if there was somebody right there. I turned to look at the passengers seat to see if anyone was there. As I was driving the scent became stronger and stronger. The smell started to become quite overpowering. I remember my kids asking me if I had spilled a bottle of perfume in the car. My son had said that this smells awful and started to make these silly noises as boys sometimes do. The scent became so strong that I was becoming nauseated. I pulled down the windows to let some air in, however, the scent did not disappear. It became so pungent that I had to pull the car over to the side. It was as if someone had spilled a large bottle of perfume in the passengers seat!

I recognized the scent as the perfume Aunt Doreen used to wear and I knew she was with us. Perfumes on people smell different depending on their body's chemistry. This scent smelled exactly as she wore it. And she knew I would recognize her by that. I just sat in the car chatting with my children with the windows opened. The scent began to die down so I started the engine back up again to get on the road, as soon as I did that the scent became so overpowering that I had to turn off the engine again. It was then that I knew she was warning me not to drive at this moment. The entire time I could feel my aunt's presence in the passenger's seat. I could not see her—but I felt her completely. This was not a frightening experience at all, but one of love and guidance. I sat there for about fifteen minutes and the scent then began to disappear. When I could no longer smell it I started the engine up and carefully began to drive. Even though the smell of perfume had dissipated, her presence did not. I knew she was still with me.

I drove very cautiously, I was feeling a bit unnerved—I wasn't sure what to expect. I knew in my heart that it was safe to go on, as I could not smell the scent anymore. As I drove along the road, I approached a bend, as I went around the bend, which was about two miles from where I had stopped the car, I saw a big pile-up of cars crashed into each other. English roads are not very wide. This was a two-lane road and with the weather not cooperating it did not make it much easier. My kids and I would have been in the middle of it as we were driving within the time period of when this accident took place. We would have definitely hit the car pile-up head on, especially since this occurred right after the bend. We would not have had a chance to brake.

I believe that my aunt saved our lives—we would been seriously injured otherwise. I believe that angels come in all forms—and that sometimes a loved one will be just that angel who watches over us. Sometimes they come to us for a short period of time and at other times they stay for our entire lifetime. I have come to understand that we are continually guided from unseen sources. And I accept shades of gray—I think when we shift our attitudes to either black or white, we lose so much of what is truly out there. When one lives with such rigidity—one tends to live in ignorance and judgment. I have no doubt that we are not in this vacuum that most of us think we live in. There are so many more things going on and just because we cannot see, feel, hear, touch or taste it, does not make it unreal.

I feel that when one really needs help, help will come from unseen corners as it did for me. I felt so at peace knowing that she was looking out for my children and me. I felt that even through her death I really never lost her—she was still around all of us, only coming to us from a different level in a different form. It was a lovely blessing to have her watch over us—very comforting.

I believe time and time again, that we are being helped from the non-physical world—only many of us are not aware of it. We tend to brush it of as coincidence or just being lucky, but do not appreciate the essence of the act. I have learnt to try to be more cognizant of my senses and more mindful of other things that are happening in my life. When we live close-mindedly—even when it is not done deliberately—we lose and miss so much of what is out there. And what a shame it is with the little planet time we have, to live within our barriers and not beyond them.

Thought 42

When thoughts of loneliness and depression arise and you think that no one in this physical world truly cares, remember: *we are never alone.* There is always someone watching from the 'other side'. You may call them your guardian angel, divine being, or loved one, but they have been with you since birth. They are beings with a spiritual force of energy, always with you in joy, tragedy, and the simple day-to-day moments. They are your ethereal mentors.

Their function is to guide you through life, making sure never to interfere with your free will. They are here to aid in some choices that are best for you in this lifetime with your karma. They give a boost here or an impression there. It can be the difference between taking an easy or bumpy road. Just because one road is easier, does not make it the wrong choice.

When you feel isolated—call to them, ask to be surrounded by their divine presence. One way is to ask for a white light to encircle your body. Envision it in your third eye, while in meditation or when you engage in *quiet time*.

* * *

This story came to me from a woman named Rae-Ann, who was diagnosed with a brain tumor in August of 1997. This is a remarkable story of strength and courage, intertwined in the phenomenon of human order versus divine order. Many reading this story will ask if this really happened. I say to those who do, to go beyond the miracle and focus on the lesson learned. *For it is in the lesson that the miracle lies.*

This is Rae-Ann's story:

Thirteen months prior to my surgery I would have seizures (which at that time I did not know were seizures). Every time a seizure would start I would feel a presence, it felt like something or someone was behind me. The minute I turned to see who it was, I would feel this presence moving out of my view. I have no doubt that there was some type of energy around me; it was too strong to ignore. I believe that it was either a guardian angel or some spiritual force. When my seizures would take place, I never fell or was in a position of helplessness. They never occurred when I was at work or driving, always in the safety of my home. At that time the doctors did not know what this was, they diagnosed as a pinched nerve in my back.

August 13, 1997, was my son's birthday and this is where I had a big seizure. I ended up in the hospital, where a few tests were done and nothing was found. I was told to go see my physician, who then ordered additional tests.

My test results came back and my doctor showed me the tumor on the X-ray; to me it looked like the size of a baseball. It was in between my skull and brain; it was called a Menningeoma tumor. I was scheduled for surgery September 4, 1997, at 7:30 a.m. In the meantime, I was given medication to control seizures.

My manicurist told me of a client named Pamela, who had been through what I was about to go through, a benign tumor and surgery. I called Pam up and we met. It was through Pam that I learned how to meditate. She came to my house and brought with her materials on meditation and how the mind-body connection works within each of us. I became aware of the energetic system that each one of us carries and how we have the ability to tap into this richness.

Although not familiar with meditation, I felt that this would be very helpful towards a positive recovery. By learning how to meditate, I became aware of my inner being, my soul. I became aware of the power of mind over body. I learned creative visualization, which is another mode of meditation. I would picture myself on the day of the surgery, packing for my trip to the hospital. I then would picture myself surrounded by loved ones as they wheeled me off to surgery. Finally at the end, I would see myself coming out of the surgery alive, well and in harmony with my body.

Waiting can sometimes be the hardest part of the process, as it was for me. Being home for ten days before the surgery was extremely difficult, but through meditation and visualization I became stronger inside. By working on the internal Self, I was able to handle the external environment better. I had a mantra that I would concentrate on and with that I would feel my mind, body and spirit blend together as One.

I am a firm believer in the power of prayer and positive thinking. I believe our thoughts give great credence to the lives we live. I began what you might call a national prayer chain. I asked family, friends, and everyone they knew who believed in the power of prayer and positive thinking, to include me in their thoughts on September 4, 1997, at 7:30 a.m., the time of my surgery.

I arrived at the hospital at 5:30 a.m. accompanied by my family. I had some positive affirmations written down which I would repeat as my mantra. They wheeled me to where I was to be prepped for surgery. There must have been about twenty-five people there. I just remember thinking that my life was in their hands. I kept repeating my affirmations, but deep, deep down, I was scared. The nurses were introducing themselves to me and the last thing I remember before surgery was a nurse telling me that she was going to give me the anesthetic.

I went into intensive care after the surgery and was feeling quite dizzy. I was trying to open my eyes, but could not due to the intensity of the bright light.

I remember a lady coming to my side and saying *"Rae-Ann, do you remember me?"*

I opened my eyes and saw this most angelic face. She had blonde hair, was heavy set, and pretty.

I just shook my head and said *"No"* and closed my eyes again.

She said, *"well, I held your hand during your surgery and yours is a miracle surgery."*

I opened up my eyes again where she gave me the thumbs up saying, *"keep up the good work,"* and she left. I woke up hours later remembering that nurse and what she had said. I thought to myself what a wonderful hospital, how nice of them to have someone come in and hold my hand throughout the surgery. My surgery lasted four hours and this nurse was present the entire length. I believed that this was standard procedure; I had no idea that it was not.

Afterward, I was moved to a room and every time a nurse would come in to take my vitals, each one commented on how amazing my recovery was. One by one, an IV or a tube was removed. Each nurse told me that I was the only one on the floor who had vital readings that perfect. The physical therapist came to take me for a walk. She said that by standard recovery definition, physical therapy was needed, although in my case she could not see where any was necessary.

They allowed me to go home, but I maintained regular visits to the doctor as aftercare. I had fifty-three staples in my head that needed to be removed, among other things, so my visits were frequent. I was told that I still needed to take my seizure medication for six months, but four weeks after surgery the doctor weaned me off it. The doctors had informed me that it would take three to six months of complete bed rest. Ten weeks after my brain surgery, I was out driving and Christmas shopping.

Basically life went on and I was living a normal happy existence. In six months I had to go back and get another MRI evaluated.

I had my MRI and my doctor said to me in his charming accent, *"You have a beautiful brain. It looks like you never even had surgery."*

I left my doctors office and decided to see the nurses to say hello, as they were so sweet to me. I met with all of them and then I saw the nurse that came to visit me from intensive care.

I said *"Oh, excuse me I don't know if you remember me or not, but six months ago I was here to have brain surgery and you told me that you held my hand and that it was a miracle surgery."*

She turns and says to me, *"Rae-Ann"*.

I said, *" Oh, you remember me."*

She replied, *" I remember every second of your surgery, I'll never forget it for as long as I live."*

I said, *"really, why... is that the first brain surgery you have seen."*

She said, *"No... but it was the first miracle surgery I've seen. I am the Director of Nursing for the Neurological Surgery department, and randomly, from time to time, I will go in to observe different surgeries to keep abreast. I read over your case, and I asked your doctor if I could observe your surgery. I received clearance and was given permission to watch. I do not know why, but I felt compelled to be there. I was in surgery with you and yes, I did hold your hand. I kept telling you that you were doing a great and wonderful job."*

When I heard this, I kept thinking to myself this is exactly what I prayed for, no negative thoughts. I wanted all positive energies surrounding me that day. She was the answer to my prayers.

She began tearing as she continued; *" I held your hand and saw right inside your brain. First they shaved your head and then they cut a piece from your skull and set it aside. It was then that I was able to see your tumor. When the doctor saw the tumor he said, 'she will have many residual deficits because of this tumor'. No sooner did those words leave his mouth, when I witnessed a phenomenon. The room lit with hundreds of angels hovering over you and tending to you. That is when I knew that I was witnessing a miracle and that's when I knew you were being healed. You know, I recount to my nurses what I saw that day when I'm teaching. I tell them about this wonder that I was blessed to witness."*

I immediately felt that this was God's way of answering my prayers. It was very important for me to have positive thoughts infiltrate the surgery room. It was very meaningful for me that the room be filled with energetic healing and love. I believe that there was a reason she was there. I have no doubt that she was there to bear witness in order to relay it back to me at a later time. I thought once more of the presence I felt at my side prior to each seizure and could not help but think that may have been an angel— perhaps my guardian angel?

I have now become more aware of life's subtleties. I am more attuned into how divine intervention works and how there are never really any coincidences. I now believe there is a master plan at work. I have come to believe the lessons we might need to learn will be shown to us in ways that God feels is best. We may not feel so at that time, as each one of us masters life's experiences differently. However, our soul does not take on more than we can handle. These lessons will be given to us in the best way that we can master and grow, and in the time where we might appropriately receive them.

I am grateful each day for things that I used to take for granted; a body which functions without impairments and the energy it takes to get daily tasks accomplished. I wake up every day with an immense amount of thankfulness and indebtedness for my life. I appreciate the sense of awe that comes over me when I hear the wind rustling through the trees. To listen to the morning melody of birds chirping amongst nature is now a daily gift from the heavens. I am appreciative of time. I am especially thankful for His messengers of love, who each day promote healing and love on our planet through seen and unseen ways.

Thought 43

Is it really possible, divine intervention? Yes! It comes as a *knowing-ness* you feel within, but do not know why. It may appear as the little voice that warns you when you have gone astray. It can speak in ways that may not seem your own, yet *trust, listen, and accept,* for only then can two-way communication commence.

A first idea or thought that may emerge from *no where* will come from the Universe through non-physical guides, teachers, and masters. It will appear so clear, feel so right, that you will have marveled at its formation and focus. Do not question, revise, or distrust the connection. If you have doubts—that is good, for then it surely was not from you!

Our Higher Self

"When the state of dreaming has dawned,
Do not lie in ignorance like a corpse,
Enter the natural sphere of unwavering attentiveness.
Recognize your dreams and transform illusion into luminosity.
Do not sleep like an animal.
Do the practice which mixes sleep and reality."

Tibetan Buddhist Prayer

Thought 44

Why is it necessary to focus inward in a society that is based outward? The search to find our Higher Self is emerged within a battle of two polarities; the inner and outer dimensions. While the inner dimensions concentrate on meditation, self-analysis, and dream interpretation, the outer dimensions are nature relationships and service in the material world.

We should be aware that from time to time, our Higher Self is seen through the voices of others, or through the beauty of mother earth. This can happen when we are taking a walk, gardening, or looking at the sunset. The feelings that transpire from within are your Higher Self. When one feels "inspired" it is actually the Higher Self communicating through the presence of nature.

The same can be said through relationships. We might hear something that hits a chord within us and gives us the answer we have been searching for, but this voice may come from a friend or acquaintance unknowingly. This is one of the many ways in which our Higher Self communicates to us, in order that we may comprehend and find the answers we have been searching for.

Service is another form in which our Authentic Self is made manifest. When we give in the truest sense, expecting nothing, a reflection of our Atman (who we are), which has been hidden within the depths of everyday survival, emerges. This again is our Higher Self.

The path to Oneness is an opening within both worlds.

* * *

This story comes from an experience that I encountered one summer night in 1999 while driving to meet my husband and some friends for dinner. In one brilliant second a flash of emotions occurred that allowed me to take a look at who I really was—and not what I thought I was.

This is my story:

I was driving along I-75 north to meet my husband and two friends for dinner at a local country club in Flint. I was running slightly late by a few minutes but hoped to make it on time. About fifteen minutes into my drive I saw a small car smashed in the median that was a deep ditch between the two highways. There were just a handful of people who stopped—and it looked like this had just occurred a few minutes ago. I saw a girl lying a few feet away from the car and two men trying to help her. For some reason I decided to stop and see if I could help. I went straight to the girl, kneeled behind her and held her head firmly so as no movement could occur to further any neck injuries.

I said to myself, *"God, she looks no older then eighteen years of age."*

She seemed to be in and out of consciousness. I remember her looking at me when she awoke with eyes that searched for security and answers. She started to panic and scream. I bent over and whispered that it will be okay and not worry as I tried to stroke her forehead while maintaining a tight hold of her head. She seemed to calm down as she looked straight into my eyes, never leaving my view. The ambulances had not come and more people began to gather around the accident. A witness, who was behind her, told me that she lost control of her vehicle and was thrown from her car.

A crowd of individuals began to gather around the accident scene. I began to notice a few muffled voices and people looking in the direction of the girl's car. Smoke started to arise from the car and I remember seeing people backing away up the hill.

I turned my head to hear a man's voice say, *"Run! The car is going to blow!"*

I turned quickly to see the car begin to flame. I looked down at this young girl who obviously was not going anywhere and thought to myself, *"shoot, I better get the hell out of here—but what about her?"*

It's funny how many thoughts stream through your mind in a millisecond. I have heard people say that their life flashes before their eyes. I now have a small understanding of what that means. I looked up to see that everyone had backed away except for two individuals and myself. I began to get up and leave as well, when I noticed that these two individuals seemed unconcerned about the fire, the car blowing up or the commotion that surrounded them. Their attention was solely on the young woman. I could not help but be mesmerized by the essence of their focus. They were more concerned about the well being of her than of anything or anyone else. It was in that second, when I was midway up and ready to do the ten-meter dash to safety, that I looked at who I was and what was life really about.

I remembered saying to myself, *"what are you doing Samira, how can you just leave her?"*

It was a bizarre moment in my life, because I came to realize that in the crunch of things, I was not ready to go the full mile and surrender my fears in order to aid another. So many things passed through my mind, it was hard to believe that one could contemplate so many scenarios within those fractions of a second. Thoughts such as, *if I stay, how badly burnt will I be? How can I protect myself and this girl from the debris of the car when it explodes? What will happen if I my face incurs some burn injuries?*

These were just some of the thoughts that raced through my head. It is ironic how the divine presents to us these situations, and how each one of us handles it on an internal and external level. For myself, it was more of an "*I*" dilemma—of which I came to terms with within those seconds of deciphering what to do. Although I was concerned with how to help or move this young girl to safety—I was more concerned about the "*me*".

After all the fears had made their way through my mind—I remained with this young woman and these two other individuals. A part of me could not leave or live with myself if something was to occur. And it was in those moments that a portion of my fear began to surrender and it was then that I left it up to God. I kneeled back down, whispered to her that she was doing fine and gently stroked her forehead. A few minutes later a policeman came with an extinguisher and dissolved the flames from the car. I saw two paramedics come to where we were, so I got up and allowed them to do their job. I walked up the ditch of the median to my car and drove away.

Thought 45

It is through intuition that reality begins. Intuition impels us to go beyond our limitations and accept a truth with complete assuredness. We acquire this information without physical evidence. Sense it to be true, without having full comprehension of how we discovered it, yet we are confident of its certainty.

This is the glory of the inner dimensions. This richness is available to anyone who can close the doors of rational assumption and expose their mind to a transcendent knowledge where foundation stems from second sight.

* * *

This story comes from my husband Vikram. It is a story that goes beyond the thin veil that shields one dimension from another. The spirit of this experience summons us to keep an open mind to some of life's mysteries.

This is Vikram's story:

Approximately two weeks before my father passed away, I had two dreams on two consecutive nights that my father had a heart attack and died. The dreams were pretty much identical in that the message was very clear. I do not remember where it took place or what I did in the dream, but I awoke up in the middle of the night panic stricken from these mental images.

I remember saying to myself, *"Thank God that it was just a dream."*

At that time, the only thing that struck me odd was that it occurred two nights in a row and with such clarity and distinctness.

Being in the medical profession, the metaphysical world has played little significance in my daily life. Although I found myself having the capacity to become more open, I did not interpret those dreams as anything but horrible nightmares—despite my intuition.

I have learnt quite a bit from my father's passing, however, the biggest thing that I have taken from his death is that there are times when I am definitely more in touch with the infinite flow of life—the Universal truth. Those are the moments in my life when I feel most connected, peaceful and strong. At other times, when I am not as connected the normal human emotions come into play, such as anger, fear, and insecurity. It has become easier for me to recognize when I am in touch and when I am not. I guess the next step is to become more attuned more of the time than not.

With my father gone, I was able to receive a glimpse of the birth and death cycle. I was able to finally recognize that despite death, there are other planes of consciousness, and that we can all have the opportunity to communicate with each other through these various levels. I have begun to observe and understand this cycle and its meaning. I have found that by becoming less bound to the norms of conventional thought, I am better able to receive a clearer perspective on what is important in the short time that we have; and the purpose each one of us brings when we incarnate. Not to say that I am doing all of that, but to say that I have some understanding of that now, where previously I might not have had.

I am learning not to readily dispute something just because I may not believe in it. By maintaining an open attitude I have become less judgmental. Certain concepts that I found difficult to decipher in the past have now become easier to perceive—possibly because I am allowing myself to go beyond what I cannot see, hear, touch, taste, or smell.

I have observed that persons, who are much more sensitive to these various levels of consciousness, are better able to communicate and receive information from their own super-conscious. I was given a momentary view of this and I would like to see if I could receive more. This glimpse came from a third dream concerning my father. The last week of February, I experienced a very vivid dream of which I felt it contained complete truth.

My dad had come to me and I remember looking at him and asking, *"what are you doing there now to keep you busy?"*

He looked at me and said, *"I am here welcoming people up from earth when they die and move on to the next plane of life"*.

From what was shown to me, I came away with a strong sense that my dad was also helping transition individuals who had passed on from heart attacks to their new home. This specific dream was even more intense than the heart attack dream, as I felt that I was in a different place. It was exceptionally unusual than just a regular dream. I actually felt that I was in an altered plane of existence, not just the regular dream-state. I encountered love emanating from his presence to me— somewhat like the process of osmosis. It was as if I felt what he felt for me.

When I awoke from the dream it was at that point that I knew that my brother-in-law's mother would not make it. I know this sounds slightly off, but it was similar to a vision being played out before me. My brother-in-law's mother had gone in for routine surgery, complications arose and she ended up in critical condition. I remember telling my wife right after I had the dream that she was going to pass on, and that dad was going to be the one welcoming her to the next plane of life. A week later she died.

Before my father passed on, I lived life out of fear, always afraid of what if this or that did not happen. This fear was the foundation of anger, jealousy—and all those similar emotions. There was a time right after my father's death that I was the most peaceful— very few of life's trivialities bothered me. I began to live my existence in gratitude—waking and ending the day with a sense of contentment within and without.

Over time, there have been days when I have found myself slipping back into my old self—and in those instances I try to seek clarity in Being. In this state of Self-remembering, I am relearning that acceptance is transcendence. I am learning that nothing is permanent—so in order for me to exist within the flow—I must become the flow. In doing so, I must embrace my pain, depression, and fear. Consequently, I allow the natural process of change to transform itself. This permits me to remain indifferent and detached—knowing that this state of mind will pass—as does everything else in life.

Thought 46

When a dream is so authentic that you can actually feel the presence of that person you are dreaming about, it is real; only it is taking place at a different level of consciousness. Dreams talk to us through our thought process; this type of communication is the Higher Self guiding our path. When we see someone clearly, or we hear words with such clarity, this no longer remains a dream, but is our inner reality speaking on another plane of existence.

Beyond the ego and barriers of our five sensory worlds the Self breaks through to converse in the language it knows best, *the dream process.* However, not all dreams have meaning: some work over the days past images from our unconscious. You will be able to discern which to discard, for its power will enfold you.

Being in body is not the highest part of who we are, the highest part belongs to our Higher Self, which communicates to the astral plane through our super-conscious. If you wake up and remember your dream, it is because you were meant to. If you wake up with a strong sense that the dream was in some way meaningful, this is because it was meant for your ears. This is one of many ways in which the Universe communicates to us.

* * *

This story comes to me from Teresa L., a volunteer and friend who I became acquainted with in a charity organization where we both are members.

This is Teresa's story:

My sister Josie passed away when she was thirty-seven: at that time I was thirty-five. She was chronically ill most of her life. Much of her time was spent in and out of hospitals.

My sister and I were very close growing up. We shared a relationship that was somewhat telepathic. I remember one incident when I was on a ski trip and I had dislocated my shoulder. Josie was picking me up from the airport and upon arrival she asked me how my shoulder was doing. I had not called home to tell them what had happened; she just knew that I had dislocated my shoulder. There were other times when I would finish thoughts for her and she for me; we completed each other's sentences.

I was away on vacation when my sister died. In fact I cut our vacation short, as I felt a strong urge to be home that Wednesday. It was quite strange, but as our plane touched the ground to land, I could clearly hear my sister say good-bye to me. Phenomenon like this is very difficult to explain, but her voice was distinctly audible and she was saying good-bye.

I was coming home to take care of my sister in hospice care as she was being sent home from the hospital to die. My sister decided to discontinue her treatments and the doctors said she would have three to four weeks to live. As soon as I arrived back, I got into the car and started on my way to the hospital. I telephoned my mother to let her know that we were home.

My mother, not knowing I was driving said, *"Teresa... Josie just passed away".*

At that moment I realized with despair that I would never be able to see her one last time, or have the chance to say goodbye. I was very troubled and disturbed by this and could not sleep for days. The sleepless nights turned into weeks and I saw myself becoming very angry. I was blaming every body and anybody for my not being there, but most of all I blamed myself.

About six weeks later, I was in Colorado on a ranch. Although I was active throughout the day and very exhausted by nightfall, I still had difficulty sleeping. One particular evening, I did manage to fall into a deep slumber by my husband's account. In this deep sleep state I found myself sitting and talking to my sister. In spite of the fact that this appeared to be a dream, it felt too authentic.

Over the period of her last year, my sister had lost a lot of weight, her eyes were hollow, she was extremely pale and her hair was thin. In this *"so called"* dream, I was carrying my sister down a mountain; we were at twelve thousand feet elevation. I used to carry her when she was alive, as she had episodes where she was too ill to walk; Josie was a small girl. Well, we were walking down a trail and my sister told me that she did not care that I was not present when she passed on. However, I just kept babbling on about how sorry I was that I was not there at the end.

I put Josie down to look up at the mountains we walked down from. I told her how beautiful the mountains were as the sun was just beginning to set.

We were looking at the sun setting over the Rockies when I said, *"I just love the mountains"*.

She was standing next to me and I repeated, *"aren't those mountains beautiful"*.

We were on a rough sidewalk and there was a gravel road. I turned to see her, as she was on my right side and it was at that moment that she transformed. She looked like she did in her early thirties. Her face had a healthy fullness to it; her hair was thick and abundant, while her eyes expressed brightness. She had her makeup on, like she did when she was alive. She looked radiant!

I expressed to her in the dream how I was feeling with the guilt and unhappiness about not being there for her when she crossed over.

Josie told me that I should not feel this way, she said *"Don't worry about it Teresa, it is over"*.

She smiled and said, *"Teresa, I am going to be alright, really"*.

At that moment a car pulled up, it was a red convertible, something that my sister definitely would have driven. I looked at the guy in the car who was coming to get her. He had dark wavy hair and a big smile that looked right at me. He smiled with a certainty that I should know who he was. It seemed that I should have known, yet I could not place him. In the back seat there were two women who also looked very familiar, yet I could not place them either.

He smiled at me and put his hand on my hand as it rested on the car. He looked at me and said with certitude, *"Don't worry we are going to be <u>All</u> right"!*

Josie then got into the car, shut the door and said, *"I have to go now"*, and drove off.

I remember watching puffs of dust trail behind them as they drove away. I turned to walk back up the mountain and this is when I awoke. Upon awakening, I knew this was not a dream, I felt dusty and my arms were weak like I had been carrying some weights. It was too vivid to be a dream. Believe me I know dreams. Usually they are broken up into different thought patterns, still, what I experienced was unique yet extraordinary. I never had an experience like that since.

That morning when I woke up, my husband commented that I must have slept well

I said *"I didn't sleep at all, I am exhausted'.*

He said, *"you were snoring, you seemed to be in a deep sleep."* I replied, *"I don't feel like I slept at all, my arms are killing me."*

The strangest thing is, about a month or so later, my sister's best friend had a very similar experience where she spent an evening with Josie. She recalled that she felt that she did not sleep also, yet her husband said that she slept through the night as well.

It has been eight years since I had that experience and to this day I know that I was with my sister up in the Colorado Mountains. I feel that my sister allowed me to release my anger, guilt, and unhappiness of not being there. I know that there was a reason for me not to be there before she passed and I now have accepted and released it.

When I worked as an R.N. especially in the Oncology units, I would remark to my colleagues that certain patients' times were drawing near where they would pass shortly. I would feel a presence in the room of the patient and knew instinctively that somebody would be coming for them. On several instances, I would walk into the room and witness a shadow of someone by the bed. I would walk away and know that this person would die, even if they were not expected too. It usually happened within twenty-four to forty-eight hours after I had walked into their room. My sister also had several similar experiences. She used to work in camps for children with cancer, many of the kids would relay to her that there was somebody in the room. They would ask her if they should go with them.

My sister would reply, *"yes— I think you should go with them"*, and then the children would soon pass over.

At one point, when we knew my sister would not live very long, I had said to her that I wanted to be there with her before she crossed to the other veil of life. I now believe circumstances had it for me to be absent when she died. Since the dream, I now know that my Uncle Frank, the man in the dream that I did not recognize, was the one who came for Josie. The man in the car was about thirty-two years old; I never saw Uncle Frank look so young as he was forty when I was born. It was not until several years later, when I was browsing through an old family album, that I saw a picture of my Uncle Frank in his early thirties. I remember thinking what an uncanny resemblance to the man in my dream with Josie. It was soon confirmed that it was him.

I know and believe that Josie assisted in helping me to extinguish the guilt, anger, and unhappiness I was carrying since her death. Her visit in my dream began the process of healing. Soon afterward, I found myself being able to sleep again. I believe she was trying to convey to me that after one dies, the earthly concerns that consume us with worry, anger, and guilt, destroy so much of who we are. A part of what shapes our soul is time and how we manage the minutes and seconds allotted to each of us individually. Her message to me was to learn to let go—love—and live.

A Path to Self-Realization

"All you need is already inside you, only you must approach yourself with reverence and with love. Self-hatred and self- distrust are grievous errors. Your constant flight from pain and search for pleasure is a sign of love you bear for yourself. All I plead with you is this; make love of yourself perfect. Deny yourself nothing. Give yourself infinity and eternity, and discover that you do not need them. You are beyond."

Nisargadatta Maharaj

Thoughts 47

Who am I? A question we must continually ask ourselves. We are the Atman (inner divinity). How does one go to our Atman (inner divinity)?...through the realization of the Self. This super-conscious is the essence of God.

When we understand that divinity lives inside of us, we need not seek outward, as solutions are within each of our soul's heart, ticking one beat upon another—as questions become answers.

Only when we can grasp the 'I' can we then discern the 'Am' (cosmic consciousness). When we are able to master the concepts of ego, attachment, and desire, we come to understand the 'I'. It is then that we can merge the 'I' with the 'Am' - making the mantra 'I Am' our essence, being, and consciousness.

However, when this awareness becomes complete the existence of 'I Am' will cease and one will reach a state of samadhi (known-ness, Divine consciousness). At this level one will absorb All without having the need to perceive. In this think-less state, we will not look for answers outside of us. We will finally reach a state of Being, where we come to know that we are the answer.

Thought 48

What is meant when we refer to the heart? The heart in the spiritual parlance has no flesh and is not a component of our human body. The spiritual heart is a formless presence that lies in every human being, animal, and plant regardless of misdeed or evil. It is omnipresent and changeless. It lies in the chest area and also in every other part of who we are— it is infinite.

True freedom is achieved through recognition and realization of the heart. One need not be an elder or sage to attain it. Liberation can take years or evolve over milliseconds—it depends on how attached we are to suffering.

Thought 49

When we think of the term Self-realization many picture an immaculate state of consciousness, which is difficult to attain. This interpretation is an invalid belief. Self-realization is not something that is earned or that is arduous to achieve. Self-realization is really Self-actualization. We actually awaken ourselves to our soul's reality, wisdom, and inexpressible mystery of who we *always* were and what we have *always* been.

Thought 50

As adults raising the next generation communication between ourselves and our children play a vital role in developing their *Self.* When we raise our voices, argue or become violent due to unresolved issues between our partner and within ourselves—we capture a precious part of our children's childhood. We peel a part of their security and esteem and replace it with fear and unpredictability.

When alcohol, anger or the like become uncontrolled—we convey to our children that their needs for stability and nurturing will not be met. This is one of the most selfish acts many individuals do. The entire adult system of energy is being fed into a dangerous ego, while the children are left to fend for themselves.

If adults realized how attuned children are and how their sensitivity level is often more acute and heightened than that of their own—maybe a second thought would be given when words are voiced with alcohol and actions implemented with anger. The connection children have to God before they reach teen-hood is often times free from being inhibited by outside influences—thus, allowing for elevation of their awareness and extra sensory perception.

We all have incarnated for a purpose and life begins when we recognize what that purpose is. Children need guidance in finding out who they are and what their intent may be on this earth. Yet, many children grow into adulthood with their ears opened outwardly, rather than focused inwardly.

For many, substance is lacking—and they find themselves plugging into a vast array of areas, except the one that could summon the greatest contentment. This realm is the path of *who they are.* And this journey is the most arduous of all life's obstacles. Yet, when found—it remains the salt of our soul.

Thought 51

What is meant by the phrase; remembering who we are and where we came from? To remember who and where we came from, we must first go beyond the eyes of birth. This is a state of consciousness where, at the shedding of our bodies, awareness will encapsulate the soul like that of a membrane. It is within this membrane of memory that our mindfulness heightens. This will cultivate further understandings that will relate back to the development of our soul-truth.

This is where, on some level, life's mysteries are unveiled and expansion and growth continues. However, expansion and growth should not be suspended for our deathbed. It is in the here and now—in the every day—that we have a chance and a choice to learn how to unlearn and evolve the spirit born within each of us.

We each carry this awareness before we incarnate and children particularly, retain some of this in their early years. What may seem as imaginary friends, in some cases may not be so imaginary at all? Children often experience the presence of guardian angels, loved ones, or spiritual guides, and tend to have little or no barriers. Their perception and innocence leads them to see truth with their eyes open, in comparison to most adults who walk with barriers as thick as cement blocks.

As we grow our remembrance begins to fade and we find ourselves caught up in 'living and surviving'. However, the memory of why we came here, our purpose and who we really are, is sown deeply within our soul's vault. Those who allow themselves to embrace a more open-minded, non-judgmental attitude— increase their sensitivity. By augmentation of their sensitivity, their awareness increases and with increased awareness—the vault slowly begins to unlock.

Thought 52

What is the difference between spirituality and religion? Spirituality is based on an individual consciousness, while the foundation of religion is on a collective consciousness. This does not authorize one over another or reveal that someone who is religious is not spiritual. It does, however, state that spirituality is embedded in the roots of a Universal Oneness. This is a framework where tolerance is non-existent, and acceptance is a major component to its composition. The Upanishads and Vedas declare that truth is One—it is God—and it is omniscient and omnipresent. One needs only to unveil the inborn sanctuary within our own hearts— leaving one to experience direct actuality from a pure heart rather than a limited intellect.

Nonetheless, one can consider themselves to be religious and display little or no spirituality. This lack is due to attitudes of judgment and rigidities within their own belief system. Spirituality delves into a truth that exists within itself, a truth that lays on the foundation that has no boundaries or borders, where one does not confine him or her Self to customs, rituals, or dogmas. Spirituality welcomes anyone. It does not care if one wears a japamala (prayer beads) or a cross around one's neck. Its essence is simply unity in diversity.

As Sri Sathya Sai Baba says, "Love all Serve all".

Thought 53

What is Dharma?

Dharma is freedom unbounded in the reigns of truth; unfortunately, there is no true definition in the English language that can fully equate Dharma. Dharma is the definition of spirituality, while spirituality is the thoughts and actions implemented throughout our lives.

Dharma includes all and excludes none. Dharma has no room for ego, narrow-mindedness, and selfishness. Its stream permeates truth through experiential Oneness and bliss of the Atman, (inner divinity) and not by humankind's dogma, perception, and fear.

Dharma does not promote one belief over another— its essence is Universal Thought. It discourages sectarianism as this includes only a limited number of people. Dharma's esprit states that, as humans experiencing a fraction of what the Universe is, we cannot therefore, embed borders and limitations where truth is concerned.

As the philosopher Krishnamurthi states, "truth is a pathless land".

Thought 54

When one believes that they are at a level that many do not comprehend, they exist through their spiritual ego. I call this term the '*spirituality of ego-ness*'.

We must remember that we are all at different levels; each plane does not govern stages of higher or lower aptitudes. What these levels indicate are variances of awareness and growth within each step. We must bear in mind that the level each one finds ourselves at, is because we are comfortable in that stage of awareness. If we found ourselves in an awareness that we could not handle, we would reject or deny its existence.

We are all in a comprehension that we need to be at this present time in our lives. None of us can predict what will occur tomorrow, next week, or a year from now—as our consciousness continually alters. Nevertheless, at this present moment we are where we should be. However, this does not mean that our consciousness will change without will or self-effort. These two components are needed for growth to augment and stagnation to erode.

Therefore, when someone has a need to exhibit their spirituality publicly the most challenging part is yet to be conquered and that element makes up most of the circle—*ego*.

Thought 55

What is our purpose in life? Everyone to some extent has asked this question. For what purpose do we serve on this planet? Why have we chosen this body, this family, this job, and this particular way of living our life?

We are all meant in some small way to make our mark—to make a difference. Whether you are volunteering in a literacy program or are the one who always puts a smile on a customer's face, a difference will be felt inside another.

Reincarnation, karma, and purpose are all tied to the same string. We all choose the pace for our spiritual growth—there are no shortcuts to Self-mastery. There will be times when we find ourselves not understanding a particular piece of work— this could be in the form of a book we read, a program viewed, or a discussion heard.

It is in this state of incomprehension that we need to unlearn and remain open. Perhaps this was our path of understanding for that period in our life. Possibly at another point in time we may find ourselves comprehending a little more and what was perceived in the past to be of little sense, may show its clarity later.

As our true identity surfaces, we will discern the difference between personality and individuality. And as we go beyond personality and into the core of individuality, we will have less of a need to compare ourselves to others or feel better about who we are at another's expense. Certain truths will ascent and with those truths our mission in life will be revealed.

By learning, relearning and unlearning, we all end up digging in our own backyards— our small corner of infinity. It is here that the personality and the soul converge and fuse to operate efficiently on this plane, thus sanctioning equipoise and Self-mastery. And it is within this union that we find the missing treasure, which will inevitably link us to *purpose*.

* * *

This story comes from a dear friend of mine named Alisha. This story is about purpose, love, and sacrifice.

This is Alisha's story:

I feel that my life has been part of a grander divine plan. Fifteen years ago, my sister Meera was diagnosed with lung cancer. It has been twelve years since she died and the destiny of my life has been linked through her.

I came to the U.S. to visit my sister and her husband in 1973. It was here where I met and fell in love with a wonderful American man named Bill. I was twenty-three at that time and we were married soon after. The marriage lasted seven years. I was not mature or insightful enough to see what I was giving up. I was in a happy marriage with a husband who devoted his heart and soul to me. I was not looking to break up this marriage. That is why it was incomprehensible as to why I fell in love with a man who was the complete opposite of my husband. It was like being struck down with lightening— I was in love or at least at I thought so at that time.

I met Sanjay on a trip back to India. Looking back nothing could have changed my mind, as I was totally enraptured by this man's image. Everyone told me to think twice, but at that point I was not ready to listen.

Something my mother said to me awhile back when I was about to leave Bill still rings hard with me, after so many years.

She said, *"Alisha, when you break somebody's heart, you get it back in some form or another, think hard before you break Bill's heart."*

Bill was shattered and told me that I was making a terrible mistake. He said that he was willing to let this whole episode ride out. However, I felt that I was doing the right thing by following my heart and marrying Sanjay. That would be the piece that would spur the components to the rest of my life.

I married Sanjay and it took just a few months for the dazzle to wear its shine out. Sanjay never worked a day in his life, lived off of me, was abusive and to top that off, fooled around. I was working for a travel agency in New York at that time and would receive as part of my benefit package free airline tickets. Sanjay would fly out with these free passages, tell me he was going for a week and never return for about three to four months—this was the life we led.

Well, what my mother had once said to me came true, I paid double for what I did. Bill was the sweetest and kindest man I knew. He still keeps in touch with our family and to this day my mother thinks of him as a son. Looking at the big picture, however, I do not regret anything—for if Sanjay had not come into my life, I would have never left Bill. And I could have never been there for my sister's children, raising them, and eventually taking the role of their mother.

My older sister Meera was living in Toronto at the time as her husband had begun a residency program there. My younger sister Ruby, came from India for a visit and ended up staying in Toronto and living with them. The family then moved to Ohio along with Ruby. Two years after the twin girls were born, Meera was diagnosed with lung cancer. Ruby then began to help raise the girls.

I was in New York working and still in this off and on marriage. I was in a job that I was slowly dying in for twelve years. Somehow, I could not pull myself out of this rut. I was constantly complaining to Meera that I was going to quit. Meera never took me seriously as I never went through with it.

In July of 1986, Meera told me something that I have not forgotten to this day, she said, *"unless you quit your job and leave Sanjay—your life will never fall into place."*

What these prophetic words meant at that time, I had no idea. However, a divine plan was in order, even though I felt that my life was a mess.

July 1986, Meera and her family were moving back to India. Sometime around mid-August 1986, I finally said good-bye to my job. I was at the point that I could not take being in a field where I felt my purpose was being wasted—I guess you can say that I finally woke up and got enough courage to take that first step. I called Meera in India and telling her what I had just done-there was a pin drop silence at the other end—she could not believe it. She had always thought of me as someone who just complained and did nothing constructive to fix the problem. For the first time in my life, I walked that first step!

In 1983, Meera was diagnosed with lung cancer. She had surgery to remove the cancer and then went into remission. As a family we thought she was cured and on her way to recovery. It never entered our minds that the cancer would return as Meera would never bring up the subject nor want us to speak of it. Therefore, after her surgery to keep her spirits up none of us would mention the C word around her. Ruby, who had helped raise the children, especially the twins, was someone who my sister felt contented to leave them in her care if something were to happen to her. However, Ruby had fallen in love with a lovely Canadian man in Toronto and was soon to be married.

The wedding was in Ohio. The day that Ruby was to leave for Toronto I looked at Meera and although she was joyous, there was a subtle sorrow that encapsulated her appearance. I believe for Meera, Ruby was her one hope that if anything happened, the children could go to her and still maintain that feeling of safety and contentedness. She was the one who had helped raise all four of them since they were young and was literally a second mother to the twins till the age of five. As for me I was still unhappily married and living in New York. So in Meera's mind she could not ask me as I had my own problems to deal with at that time.

Meera and her family were moving back to India in 1986. They decided to live there permanently. She was to go ahead and settle the boys for the September session in school and then come back to close the rest of the affairs in Ohio. Around the first week of September, Meera had a second reoccurrence of the cancer in India. She became quite sick, however, she was determined to make a trip back to the U.S. to finish up.

She was coming back to Ohio to pack the remaining goods and leave in December of 1986. She stopped off in New York with the girls, who were four at that time, to see me. I made her get some tests done and found out that she needed to have surgery right away. Everything happened quite fast after her second surgery in October—she never fully recovered. The doctor told us that she had only three months to live.

At the same time, my bum of a husband had come back from India to try to get back with me. I kicked him out in May of 1986—given him some money and a plane ticket and told him not to come back. He shows up at the airport with my parents who came for Meera's surgery. They had not known that I kicked him out a few months back hoping never to see him again. He took this sad event as an opportunity to get back with me. My sister's surgery went ok and we took her to my cousin's place to regain her health. Meanwhile, while my sister was hanging on to every bit of strength she had, my husband was carousing New York City every night and coming home drunk. The lack of respect and concern for me, my sister and my family became the final straw that pushed me to file for a divorce. We were divorced a few months later.

I was now available to be with Meera and take care of her. I went with her to Ohio to spend sometime and also help close her affairs. In Ohio we also tried some experimental treatments, hoping that maybe this could be the one to save her life—but nothing worked. December 1986, everything was taken care of and Meera went back to India with the twins and my father. Although in her sickly state, she was determined to stop in Tiruparthi (a spiritual place where one of the most beautiful temples is in the south of India) to pray and receive guidance.

I went to Toronto to visit Ruby. By the third week of January I received a phone call from my other sister Anjali in India saying that Meera was not doing well and that I needed to come home. My heart sank. I booked a flight for the following day. I was preparing for the worst, envisioning that in these two to three weeks that I was not with her, she must have deteriorated very badly. I arrived in India, went home and the first thing that came out of my Meera's mouth was that she was now going to be better because I was here with her. I felt that I had become her life support; she would look to me for hope and laughter. I think she just wanted to have a permanent amnesia of what she was going through.

Quickly I began taking care of the children, but the girls were used to Ruby. Ruby was the one who they were familiar with. She was the one who fed, bathed and slept between them when they needed that extra motherly touch. By this time Meera was bedridden and there was no way that she was in any condition to take care of Neena and Natasha. So the following morning my sister called the twins into her room and told them that I was going to take care of them for a while, until she got better.

She said, *"Neena and Natasha, mom is sick right now and Alisha Aunty is here to help out until I get better. You must listen to her girls, as she is going to do everything for you now."*

She basically told them that I am going to feed and bathe them—and do everything that she at one time did. Indirectly, she was conveying to them that I was going to be their mother.

I remember conversations where Meera would turn to me and say, *"you know you have put your life on hold for me and because of that you have no life of your own."*

I would respond by telling her that this was where I was supposed to be—that there was no other place on earth that could take me away from her and the children. Since childhood, although Meera was fifteen months older then me, I was always there in her time of need. She would look to me for nurturing and guidance.

I remember a few nights when my sister and brother-in-law's friends would have some get-togethers.

Meera, feeling badly that I was home with her, would turn to me and say, *"Alisha, why don't you pick a tie for Amir and go with him, because you know that I can't go and I do not want him to be alone."*

I would have this awful feeling in my stomach. Being with Meera and Amir's friends made me very uncomfortable. But I did it as it made my sister happy. When I would go to some of the functions, many would look at me with the same thoughts running through their minds that it would be best if I married Amir. This thought was also pervasive throughout most of my family as well. They would look at me wistfully, hoping that maybe I would consider marrying my brother-in-law. From a cultural perspective, the sister is the next closest kin to take care of the children but to me, marriage with Amir was inconceivable. My brother-in-law and I were the best of friends—we were pals and more or less like brother and sister. It was extremely hard for me to switch that frame of mind and think of him in any other manner.

Weeks had passed and my sister's condition worsened. I never thought that my sister would die. I guess you could say that I was living in a fantasy world. Two days before her death, my sister went into a coma. I remember sitting up both nights with her and looking deeply into her face. I kept thinking to myself that there was no way she was going to die. I was waiting for the moment that her eyes would open and something would trigger her body to make the cancer to drain out.

My sister passed away two days later. Meera was always afraid of death, but the minute she passed away—I cannot tell you the expression of instant relief that was on her face. There were no words to explain it.

She had an expression that cried out, "*so is this what I was afraid of—was I afraid of this all along!*"

It was quite extraordinary!

Her four children were left in my care. The eldest son was fifteen, her next son eleven, and the twins were five. When you go through such a tragedy, one looks to divert their mind. For myself it was finishing up my sister's dream house that was in the midst of being built. The boys returned to school and we put the twins in preschool. Everything went as planned and the house was finally completed in May of that year. It was exactly as she had designed and desired. I moved into my sister's home and started to take care of my nieces and nephews. The children have always been close to me as their Aunt, but now I felt the bond intensify between us and some semblance of stability was taking shape in both our lives.

Everything was fine until the pressure to marry Amir began to take it course from family and friends a year and a half later. My sister's husband was a very conservative and traditional man, while I was exactly his opposite. As a sister-in-law, we got along just great, but as a wife, suddenly I had to become something that I was not. I took off to Toronto with the twins during their summer vacation to be with Ruby, as I needed to clear my mind. I thought very deeply about this and I went back to India a little more open to the concept that maybe this is the right thing and that the children needed not only a father but a mother as well.

I remember my mother saying, *"I think that this is the right thing for you Alisha and in time you will see that it will work out."*

Two years after my sister's death, my eldest son proposed on behalf of his father. I very emotionally said yes as something inside of me told me that it would work out. Ironically, I look back to the times before my sister became ill when I would visit her in Ohio. Amir and I used to rag and tease her so much so that she would say to us jokingly maybe we should have been married. You hear these words, think it to be funny, and then one day it ends up being your destiny—how mysterious life can be at times.

I have taken so much from my sister's death and raising her children. Before my sister died I was very afraid of death. I used to think that it was ridiculous why people went to the cemetery and why some spoke to the dead. I never believed in such things and thought it to be rubbish. However, when my sister passed on, my perspective on death and the afterlife changed completely. I would visit the cemetery along with my brothers and sisters and we would talk to Meera. We would tell her the comings and goings of what was happening with each one of us, and we could feel that she was really there listening and laughing along with us.

Even now when I go back home and visit her gravesite, I gently pat her tombstone and have regular conversations with her. I never dawns on you until something like this directly affects your emotions and your life. You become less apt to think so narrow-mindedly of others and their actions. When you hear people feeling the presence of their loved one, or smelling a particular scent that they used to wear or even communicating to them—you're not so quick to judge anymore—because you end up looking at the reflection of yourself.

I now live back in Ohio and have been married for ten years. My girls are eighteen and in college, while both sons are studying medicine on the East Coast. The greatest thing that has come out of this experience is the unending love that I have for my sister's children. I never knew that such a motherly love existed within me for another human being, let alone four of them!

I never cared nor liked children very much. I was one of those people who, when I saw other people's kids, I would not think that they were cute or sweet, only feelings of indifference would emerge. The emotions that have emanated internally for these children have become so natural. It is like a river of love that streams down a valley and then suddenly this river expands into a vaster body of water that flows endlessly. This current of love has been with me from the instant these children became a part of my life.

I truly believe that my purpose and destiny has been to raise these kids and give them a sense of family and a sense of security. Although it was doubly hard, as I got the children when they were older, I concentrated on giving them an abundance of unconditional love. From that foundation everything else was laid, sanded and cemented. I wanted these children to grow up with a passion for whatever they partook in life. I taught them that the heart never lies and that one must learn to listen to it and learn to speak from it. Even if I may not like what they might tell me—I told them that I would listen and do my best to keep an open mind.

My girls told me a story recently about a girl they know in their dorm. This girl comes from a very religious and disciplinary family background. My twins were telling me that she is acting as if she has escaped from prison. She has become a chain-smoker and tells the twins that she cannot wait to drink and get drunk. She says that she hates going home and assumed that they felt the same way. My girls said to me that this girl was so surprised when they told her that they missed being at home. They told her that yes they also had strict parents, but that they did not feel repressed or afraid, as that they were taught to speak their minds about what they felt inside. As their mother, it made me so proud to hear and to know that what I have tried to instill in them was emanating from conversations such as these.

I am continuing to discover what my purpose in life is. I still have a ways to go as the path of learning and unlearning is an endless destination. However, there are a few things that I am certain of in this life and one of those things is the importance of parenting, if one so chooses. For myself, it was and is the greatest purpose that we can accomplish as human beings. And I feel that if one were to lose sight of this—then an immense opportunity would be missed to experience an inner growth of who you are, while simultaneously encountering what it means to love another human being selflessly.

Thought 56

The deeper the emotional response, the greater the remembrance. This is called *Yearning*. It is when we are in this "emotional state" that we are most attuned to God. Think of this connection as a bright chord that shoots out from our crown chakra. The degree of brightness in the chord is the intensity of our sincerity. Unfortunately, the majority of us yearn the greatest when in distress. It seems that anxiety and anguish create a stronger impact than our response to joy.

To yearn is to increase our vibration. To increase our vibration, we must put insecurities, fears, wants and pride into this chord, giving it all to Him. In this act, we rid ourselves of debris and magnify our chord's consistency into an illumined light, making manifestation of our inner God—a reality. This is when we will completely hear the voice within—and this dimension is associated with our spiritual will.

Thought 57

Does detachment mean we should have little needs? No. We are human and to need nothing of the physical world is not possible. As spiritual beings, we have chosen to come into this plane at this time with this particular body.

If we start denying our physical and emotional requirements, we can hinder the progress we came here to make in the first place. There must be a balance of the physical, mental and spiritual - only then can we incorporate all three to counter balance each one.

Thought 58

Expectations—we all have them. Expectation and desire go hand in hand. You will find that when you least expect from a situation or an individual, this is when fulfillment comes forth. It is when expectations or desires are least met that we arrive at the door of disappointment. Try a simple exercise.

The next time you desire or expect something, go beyond justification and examine your wants. In the meditation or reflection, become detached to the desire and replace it with a question as to why this necessity is required. The answer will emerge in the whisperings of your heart. It may be something you are not ready to hear as its voice might be suppressed through rationale thinking.

However, if you listen open-heartedly, without mind and ego, an understanding will give birth inside of you. This emergence is the emanation of truth—and truth is freedom. So listen carefully and listen with clarity, for the hushed tones of your soul will always shepherd your guidance.

Thought 59

Where is God? Many would declare that he is in our hearts! I would say this to you as I have heard it from my guru. We are like fish swimming through God. God is above us, below us, around us, within us, and outside of us. We breathe, sleep and live God. Like a fish swims through water, we swim through God.

Thought 60

What eventually is the goal of realizing the Self? Are there increments of happiness as on a scale that may lead one to greater or lesser degrees of contentment?

I was once asked a question very similar to the one I have addressed above. What is the goal of all of this? Is the goal to become happy and if so, where does one go from there?

When venturing into the Self, there are no scales comparing levels of contentment and happiness. True happiness is omnipresent and is neither created nor destroyed. There are no ultimate goals that one strives to be. The goal is to *Be.* To learn all you can in order to unlearn some and relearn others.

To realize what is already there and rediscover the unknown. To tread onto a chaotic path knowing that it may be the best and surest route to follow—whereas the safest route may be just that—safe.

This is the yin and the yang of life, mirroring back the rediscovered Self.

* * *

There are two stories for this thought. The first is Mary's story of unconditional love, betrayal and the longing to find home. Her experience will take us into our own walls of imprisonment. And hopefully like Mary, we will find the gates that will escort us to where our own Self resides. And the longing to find home—will be home. Some names have been disguised for privacy protection.

This is Mary's story:

According to other people, my family resembled the Cleavers. Two perfect little children, a cat and a dog, with Ted and I living a seemingly perfect existence. Our marriage was nothing from what it appeared to be on the outside.

I guess things came to surface when my husband Ted lost his job in 1990. For a period of five weeks, he had kept it hidden from his family. He would get up in the morning and go about his usual routine. When we did find out five weeks later what had transpired, it would be a year before Ted would find work. At that point, plans for our daughter Jennifer attending college were suspended and the next best option was to attend a local community college.

I think the part that led Jennifer to anorexia was the dysfunction in our family. My being not so aware and letting him do what he was doing and not trying to change that part of it affected the family as a whole. I feel that if I had gotten out of the marriage sooner she would not have gone through this. Consequently, I still have some guilt issues to resolve.

For ten years I thought that staying in this marriage was the best answer, even though Ted had a drinking problem. The courage to end this marriage was lacking. I never had the nerve or esteem to do it and say my children and I deserve better than this.

Jennifer's symptoms of anorexia began in her senior year of high school. I really did not think too seriously of it because she lost only five or ten pounds. I thought this was not unusual—especially if you were a high school girl. The following year, in 1993, she attended community college. She was thin, but not painfully thin. Then in 1994, she got a job working as a Montessori teacher while still attending classes.

It was at this point that I started to notice a significant weight loss in Jennifer. I knew then that she was not eating and that there was something seriously wrong. She had physical ailments and symptoms where she would complain of her stomach being upset and that was why she could not eat. She would also have anxiety attacks and I think it was because I was pushing her close to the truth. When you are trying to find the truth and people get close to it they become frightened. I had her at four different gastrointestinal physicians. Every doctor we went to would be a one-time appointment, when she knew that they were getting closer to the answer, she would not return.

During these two years, I also had a teenage boy to take care of, besides my work. My daughter was at a point where she would not go anywhere without me. She would not go to the mall, store or even the library. She was angry and that anger was mostly directed at me. She would say horrible statements to me daily. Hearing I hate you or you are an awful person from your own child is devastating. She did not get along with her brother or anyone who came over as well. People would wonder and question what had changed her behavior. This was not

Jennifer. She was such a loving person. I felt that I was dealing with Dr. Jackal and Mr. Hyde.

She had two good friends who she was comfortable with and one boy whom she dated off and on. He called me one night to tell me that he got her to eat part of a chicken breast. News like that kept me surviving.

Jennifer wanted to get a nose job. I thought if this was going to make her feel better then let's do it. At that point, she was about 110 pounds and her height was 5 feet 7 inches. The nose surgery was done in October 1994 and did not go well. She ended up with an infection and the possibility of losing her nose. She was on IV antibiotics every four hours 'til January of 1995. By the end of January, her physician said that she would not lose the cartilage in her nose. Unfortunately though, the reverse affect happened after her nose surgery—Jennifer stopped eating. It was like saying the nose was O.K. but I still don't feel all right, so I am not going to eat because I need to be thin.

The house was just in an uproar. I received a phone call one evening from a woman whose daughter had also battled anorexia. I did not know her from a hill of beans, but she told me something that was significant. She said that if I was not comfortable talking to friends about this that I could speak to her. She continued by saying that if I went to this particular physician who was the director of the eating disorder clinic, he would convey to me that either you or your husband have issues that need to be worked out. And that in some cases removing the child from home may have a positive effect. Sometimes children cannot thrive at home. He sent us to a female therapist whom Jennifer went to see twice a week, I attended with Jennifer once a month as an advocate.

I asked Ted to leave in March of 1995. In July 1995, Jennifer tried to take her life. I came home from work Friday night, called her from the kitchen and when she did not answer, I went to her room. I found her in bed curled up in a little ball with her dog by her side. She had taken an array of medications that she collected from going to these doctors. I took her to the hospital where they pumped her stomach. She enrolled in a day program where she would go in at 8:00 a.m. and leave at 5:00 p.m. She agreed to do this. However, sometimes they try to fool you into thinking that they are going to cooperate, as was our case—

but they are really not cooperating. They are not sure if they want to let go of that side of them.

We moved out of our home in December of 1995, which was hard for the children, as they had grown up in this house. By this time Jennifer had stopped the day clinic and resumed counseling. I would have to drag her into the car to come to these sessions. She would make it known to me that she did not want to go and that she was doing this strictly to make me happy. She said that the counseling was not doing her any good and that she was always going to remain this way.

She had turned to me and said, *"I don't feel good—I am not going to eat anymore because I want to be thin".*

I said, *"well, if you want to be thin, then fine—but I am not going to watch you kill yourself—so you will have to leave".*

This was her mindset—very stubborn. I meant what I had said. I was at a point where I could no longer have watched it. Jennifer, at that point, was eighty-seven pounds.

However, by spring 1996, she started to improve slowly, her anxiety attacks were less frequent and she was also starting to eat a little bit more. She was not losing as much hair as she used to. Previously, she would lose big bunches and I am surprised that she was not bald. Jennifer went to the same hairdresser as I did and I would ask the hairdresser for updates— if she saw any protein coming back. I was looking for any signs that things were getting better, as a mother you wanted everything to be O.K. for your child. She continued to gain weight slowly and marked improvement came as time went on.

Jennifer had lost some very good friends during the course of that period—or what she perceived to be good friends. They basically deserted her as they could not understand or deal with what was happening. The same went with her father. He really abandoned her emotionally, as he could not understand what was happening with her. He said that he could not have a child that had this illness.

He even accused me of being anorexic. He said, *"You're anorexic".*

I said, *"what are you talking about?"*

He said, *"you are too thin".*

From that statement I knew then that in his mind it was about being thin, it wasn't about everything else that could have triggered this disease.

During the middle part of the year, Jennifer and I would take long walks together every evening when I came back from work. During these walks we would talk about everything and anything. Things had really begun to improve for her and for us. She was consistently gaining weight and was beginning to accept the aspects of herself that she was uncomfortable with.

One September evening we were doing our usual 3 1/2 mile path and as we walked past the cemetery Jennifer said something that was profound. It was almost like she did not need me anymore. And when I say 'need' I mean it in the most positive sense. We were having a good conversation as to where her life was going. When all of a sudden I had this vision—I can't explain it. I can't interpret what I saw, only that it was similar to a scene being played in front me. I just saw the two of us flying in the air joined and then separating.

I turned to her smiling and said, *"Jennifer, I just saw us separating and that means you are really O.K., you don't need me so much— you can do it without me". I am always going to be here for you—but you're O.K. all by yourself".*

She turned and gave me a hug. Today Jennifer is doing great. She works as a Montessori teacher and although she is at a healthy weight, anorexia is a disease that one manages day by day—and that is what Jennifer is doing.

I have taken so much from this experience with my daughter. I feel like I have started all over again. This episode began a rebirth for me mentally and spiritually. When the burden of worrying began to lift, I had opened new doors for myself. This inner direction gave way to a sixth sense that I always had, but never took the time to develop, nor recognize its value. An awareness blossomed inside and I now have a heightened sensitivity about my surroundings, the people I meet, and who I am.

One such experience occurred after the walk with Sarah. It was with a girlfriend of mine who I saw infrequently. She had been divorced for about five years with no plans to remarry. It was the day after her father's funeral and I brought something to her home. I had not seen her for six months, until the death of her dad. She came to the door and although it had been a few months since we last saw or spoke—she looked completely different. There was something about her that was unlike someone in mourning. Again, it had nothing to do with her emotions, rather it had everything to do with her aura. I gave my condolences to her mother and then followed my girlfriend down the hall.

She then stopped and put her hand on my arm saying, *"I've got to tell you something"*.

At the moment when she said I've got to tell you something—I immediately saw doves over her head. I know it sounds bizarre—but I saw two white doves. One head was tilted towards the neck of the other, as if they were leaning into each other.

Before she had a chance to tell me, I said, *"either you are getting married or you are in love— aren't you"?*

She then said, *"how did you know?"*

I said, *"Uh...well I am not even going to explain this because you'll think that I am wacko."*

She told me that very few people knew of their relationship as she wanted to make sure before revealing to others where it was going. She did not announce the marriage to anyone and was wondering how I found out. I never did tell her what I saw—I explained it away as having a sense.

You do an awful lot of soul searching trying to find out what your role is when things happen to people whom you love. You realize that you are only part of the quotient and not the answer. And that forces you to become introspective. Everyone in any bad situation has a part to play—and you have to take responsibility for the part that you play. Then you have to decide if you can change it and what you can do to make that transition. For me, it was taking responsibility and not feeling guilt ridden when I could not do anything more.

This experience became the turning point in my life where I learned to let go of a marriage that should have never been kept together. Our marriage was purely 'bad karma'. I did not make that much money and to walk away with next to nothing was frightening.

Nonetheless, I told my children, *"I don't know where we are going to live, but you will have a roof over your head and it might be a Sears tent—but it will be a roof."*

I have done things I would have never done before. I have taken risks to improve the lifestyle for my children and myself. I may not be there completely, but the place that I find myself in— is peaceful. I feel contentment and inner happiness in my soul. I believe in myself more than I ever did. And when things become chaotic, I take out my gratitude journal and write down five things that I am grateful for that day. It takes the focus off myself and directs it to the aspects of life that are valuable to me.

Who I spend my time with and valuing every minute has become an integral part of my existence. I try to avoid negative or superficial people and environments. I look to be around a vibration and energy level that emulates realness. Things that seemed to play a significant role in the past have now become obsolete.

Money, as an example, was more of a focus before than it is now. Although vital for survival, I realized that it could flow like a two-edged sword. If consumed by its presence, one's inner life will never reach full circle. The component of money that we need to grasp is that we need to let it go. It is essential that we open our eyes when our pockets are full and not when they are empty. When the mind is cluttered, so are the thoughts and new energy cannot flow or form as easily. Understanding that all will be provided for, as it has for my children and myself, can arise only when in surrender.

My view on spirituality has also altered. When you think you are going to lose a child, it can really turn you inside out and convey to you what is significant in life. Since I had no one to turn to, I began to look within. I became aware of this small voice. It is that irking nagging voice that won't let you forget and the voice that sometimes awakens you in the middle of the night. From time to time, its whisper would simmer below all thoughts.

I now have this confidence to rely on this voice—my inner world. There may come another time in my life, when again I will have no one to lean on, but the well of Self-love will never let me down. The divinity that is within myself is steadfast. I can always tap into it—as it is a part of who I am—and that part is eternal.

This story comes from Jennifer. Her story takes us into the battle with anorexia and the battle into finding the Self within.

This is Jennifer's story:

At about ten years of age I became very aware of what I was on the outside, probably more so than most people my age. I was constantly scrutinizing myself. I never felt that I measured up to everyone else. The blonde haired girls or the girls who had the boys who chased them on the playground, were the girls who had everything. I was very sheltered from the things in life that were supposedly enjoyable at that age, like sleepovers or playing sports.

I grew up in a family where I had a very supportive mother as a role model and a father figure who was critical. He never really allowed me to be who I wanted to be through those types of activities. If I were on the swim team, he would tell me that I was not good enough or if I was pretending to sing he would tell me to stop being silly. Consequently, what I felt inside was never allowed to be expressed outwardly. Therefore, I never dealt with that part of me, as it was stunted—held back. This led me to focus on the outside.

As I went through my middle school years and into my high school years, I was always identifying with the perfect people, thinking that they were complete because on the outside they appeared to be. I was about seventeen at that time and I always wanted to be part of a group that I felt somewhat isolated from, never feeling good enough to be with these people. My Self- image was severely distorted. At that time I would not say that I was really aware of where my thoughts were heading. I looked to other ways to fit in—destructive ways that were not appropriate at that age. I would party and stay out till all hours of the night. These were things I would do to fit into those groups of individuals.

It was at that age that I really became aware of my body and weight. I would think that maybe it was my body that was not right and that was why I didn't have a boyfriend or fit in with the "in" crowd. I was an average girl in weight but that was what I focused on. I would think to myself what are the people who pass me on the street thinking? Are they thinking that I am attractive? I was so wrapped up in what every other person thought of me, never knowing what I thought of myself.

Immediately, I did not like myself. I didn't like who I was becoming. It was at that time that I decided that I could change a part of who I was. I decided to have plastic surgery at twenty years old. I had some surgery done on my nose. I thought that if it was not my body, maybe the surgery would help. After surgery things were still not perfect. I lost weight and gained it back, had plastic surgery and that still did not do it. I said to myself what else could it be?

It was then that the eating disorder really took hold. I stopped wanting to try so hard. It wasn't as if I stopped eating consciously. It was almost like I was fighting this feeling of trying to be something I was not. I didn't like the person I was, so I was going to destruct. When I began this so-called journey, I was twenty and about 140 pounds. But slowly and surely I just stopped fighting and gave in to allowing myself to wither away, because I felt that I was not good enough. And within two months I lost 30 pounds.

I did not think about eating. I was wrought with what the outside cure was to fix my problem and bring me happiness that I still believed it could be found externally. In another two months, I reached 94 pounds. Every once in awhile I would weigh myself and see that I was losing weight. I began to notice weight was coming off without even thinking about it. So I kept doing what I was doing, which was being very aware and controlled about the food that was going into my body. I started to count what was going in my body. I would count the amount of lettuce leaves I was eating and if I put mustard on the lettuce leaves or ate them plain.

With the weight coming off, I started getting comments from the crowd I desperately wanted to be accepted by such as, *" Jen, you look perfect" or "you are thin, Jen I would love to take your body to Florida on vacation".*

Here was the confirmation I was looking for from the outside world. I was 94 pounds with literally no behind. And all these people who were the people I was not good enough for, all of a sudden were telling me that I was the perfect girlfriend and that I looked perfect. So I am getting reaffirmation to destruct myself even more—the outside world was accepting me finally. The boys that I always looked at and said to myself, "God any girl that goes out with him is so lucky" were now calling me and wanting to go out with me. I had no nourishment going into my body, but these people were supposedly telling me I was perfect. I was getting what I wanted—the outside world was accepting me, but I still was not happy. I was terribly sick.

I found myself cold and crying all the time. I was treating my mother, who was the one person in my life who was the most supportive, as if she was always wrong. I would scream and yell at her for the smallest things. I recall a time when I had asked her to go to the store and buy me something. When she brought it back, it was the wrong name brand. I ended up screaming, yelling and throwing the product, when really it was my behavior that was inappropriate. But I knew that she would love me no matter what. I knew she would stick by me no matter what.

I turned 21 years old and it had been over a year of being so deep in the throes of this disease that I found myself not knowing how to get out of it. I knew I could eat—but that was only a part of it. The food was not really the issue, because I was now questioning why I still was not happy even though the outside world said I looked perfect. All of a sudden, many of the things that I thought I would receive through this stage of perfection I was not receiving. I did not have much Self-satisfaction, because I knew what I was doing was wrong, but I did not know how to stop doing it. So I sought medical help, I went to see a psychiatrist. This mental health worker told me that I was depressed and that I had to eat two more slices of bread each day and take Prozac. This all took place after a 30-minute visit.

I walked away and said, *"No."*

What is so dynamic about this eating disorder is that the people who care about you such as my mother and the people who I worked with, would say to me, *"Well, Jenny, you just have to eat that, or Jenny, just have a bite, it's not going to kill you"*.

In their minds, their main concern was the intake of food, and for me it was the power to say no to that. They were not going to make me eat, as I was not a baby. But in reality that is what you go back to. You are a fragile individual who cannot function by herself. I could not make decisions. I would stand in the grocery store with two packs of sugarless gum of different brands and I would not be able to make up my mind which brand to buy because I was so depleted. I was in a state where I was weak from being in this state but strong, knowing that I was in control of something. What I was slowly starting to realize was that I couldn't control what other people thought of me. I could influence it to some extent, but I couldn't control their thoughts. So I was going to keep the control. I was going to be so controlled that my actions would influence them to think of me differently.

I guess you can say that I really never looked at myself and I never looked in the mirror. The big part of this whole thing was that I never wanted to see what my body looked like without any clothes on. In clothes I was fine, my clothes were baggy and I did not have to deal with looking at my flesh. The bagginess covered most of it. I was wearing a size zero and I understood that I was tiny. The day that I finally looked was probably a year and half into the disease. I had been to see my good friend Tracy at her college, who had not seen me for about four months.

She went to give me a hug where she stopped and said, *"Jen"!?*

She just looked at me with tears in her eyes.

I gave her a quizzical look and said, *"What?"*

She said, *"I can feel your bones in your back."*

It was at that moment that I felt really hideous. After arriving home the next day, I took a shower and when I got out of the shower it was then that I looked at myself for the first time with no distorted body image. The blinders that always thought I was fat or not skinny enough or looking just healthy and great were now gone. And it was here that I really *saw* who I was. I looked in the mirror and I could see every rib and every bone. When I looked at my bottom I could see clear through. I had not fat in my rear end; it was just the two bones. I sat on the floor and sobbed—I screamed for my mother, because I couldn't believe it. I couldn't believe what I was seeing in the mirror—it was the one time where I did not want to be that thin person. I made my mom look at me and that is where we had both lost it. That was when I realized that this was not a game anymore.

About a week after I had this experience with my mom, I received a letter from Tracy; my friend I had previously visited. This letter was about four to five pages in length and its contents were about the meaning of true happiness. The main context read that I was a good person and when she saw me last I seemed to have lost the spark for living that I once had. My friend went on to say that I appeared to have lost the carefree spirit for life that I previously embraced when I wasn't so involved in myself as I was now. She went on to tell me that there was an etched sadness in my smile. Tracy wrote that true happiness was not what was found outside of you. She told me that the silence of my spirit conveyed the answer. We had been friends for so long that in her letter she was equating a lot of what we had gone through together to what in the end was important. She wrote that the two of us always thought we had to fit in. She said by taking care of your insides, you will feel good about whoever you are on the outside—very little will matter because you will have a good attitude no matter what happens. The cement first before the foundation.

I remember reading it and feeling good to hear this from her, but I really did not deal with it, so I tucked it away in my drawer. About a month after I had tucked the letter away I pulled it out of the drawer. It was a time when Tracey was relocating and starting a new life for herself. I suddenly began to listen to what she was saying—I probably wanted the same. I was sitting at my desk and for the first time I truly read the contents. I didn't just read it; I *really* read it. I heard it. I heard what the words were saying to me. I knew what a good friend she was to me, and that her words were real. Her words did not spell perfection or I wish I looked like you.

Her words were, *"Jen, you've got to learn that happiness comes from inside and that no matter what you look like the real people in your life will always be there. The other people you don't need anyway. So forget them".*

I know this sounds trivial, but it was like the light switch all of a sudden turned on. And I started to become aware of how important it was to look to what you are on the inside. I was learning not to focus on the outside to give me what I thought would bring me happiness. I always assumed that it was going to come from someone else or someone's words. Well, I had heard it all and those words weren't doing it. They were making me feel worse. I started to think how stupid can these people be? How can they say I look good? I am a walking skeleton who is very sick. I woke to the notion that people are always going to have different perceptions and ideas, and that I could not control their thoughts or ideas.

What I learned is that if I stopped talking to myself so harshly and handed the power over to my soul to fill me with positive and uplifting energies—then possibly instead of living in fear, I would now begin to live in surrender. I began asking myself what is happiness to me and what will fill my heart and fill my soul? Is being a size zero really going to do it for me? At the end of the day I am still with me, when I go to bed it's me and when I wake up it's me. So, if it makes me happy to look like a skeleton and be sick and fatigued all the time, then so be it. If it makes me happy to have my hair fall out and my skin looking sallow, then so be it. If it makes me happy never to hold a utensil because my joints are so stiff and fingers cramping from little nourishment; if that is really what I want—then by all means continue.

However, if I want something more. If I want something deeper, if I want to like who I am, then that knocks this concept right out of the water, because I could not be that person anymore. If I saw someone similar in my condition on the street, I would think that person was ill and had a lot of Self-hatred inside of them.

I won't deny that it is a process. The result is that you become healthy. You look at the good in yourself and you look at the person who is kind within you, and the person that is compassionate within you, and the person who has dreams and aspirations that will bring feelings of contentment and peace inside yourself. That is the goal, but the journey that you take to get there is *time*—and that is the hardest part of it all. For it doesn't just click all at once and everything falls into place. You suddenly don't feel healthy and wonderful overnight.

I am 27 years old and I was twenty when it began. I now can say that I feel that the eating disorder was my sore, my gaping gushing wound. The infection causing it, was my Self-hatred, all my feelings of unworthiness that I had about myself. I take responsibility for what I did to myself. But I also believe a part of this stemmed from my childhood and how I was raised coming from a male role model perspective. A number of young women who have this problem are affected to some extent from the role that their father played in their life. I love my father dearly, however, I also realize that he learned to parent from his parents. I can't fault him for his role models;

nonetheless, I have realized that this is where some of my feelings about my body and my Self originated.

It has been eighteen years of growing up and having certain attitudes instilled in me, so I knew that things were not going to change so quickly, although I wanted them to. I wanted everything to get better—tomorrow. That was probably the hardest part of the disease, wanting to get better but not knowing what to do. The first thing people will say is to eat something, but that is the outside force—the external part of this illness. I had to get to a safe place inside, and then I could handle the outside stuff more appropriately. The process was healing the wound. The infection is my feelings of self-hatred and unworthiness, which I believe are gone, although I am aware of its origin. To this day, I always have to keep things in perspective. It is similar to an alcoholic—once an alcoholic always an alcoholic. I believe with anorexia the same rule applies. Since the external element is the food, it can either be your friend or your foe. It can send me back if I don't eat or send me back there if I do eat and put on weight. I must maintain my sense of grounding in who I am to recognize when I may slip back a little.

I believe for the most part that I am over it, for the main reason that I do not focus on it. I concentrate on other things, such as the loved ones in my life and my job as a Montessori teacher where I have a small chance to influence the youth of tomorrow. These children will grow up and a small percentage of them just might go through what I went through. And maybe if they hear some positive internal qualities about themselves now, it might make a difference.

I know I have to have a healthy body, mind, and spirit not only for what it will give to me but for what it will give others as well. That is the other thing about anorexia. For a long time it was all about me. You become so controlled that you don't have time to give to anybody else. It was not part of the plan and not part of the agenda. I recall a time when I missed a good friend's grandmother's funeral because it did not fit into my plans of feeding the disease. When I finally was able to give my time and my heart, it was then that I started to see what true happiness and contentment was about. The feelings that emanated from these simple acts of giving were priceless to my sense of Self.

If there was a lesson in all of this for me, it was that I unearthed a power that lay dormant within myself. I recognized that what we sometimes perceive as powerful, at times may not be, and what we sometimes think of as irrelevant or trifling, is frequently where the real strength lies. The real strength was locked away somewhere in my soul—it never existed in any other place, person or opinion. This is the paradox of life—truth and contentment need not come in big packages. It will always be there—ready for me to embrace—peeking from behind a corner when I could finally see.

I am a survivor and I made it through this illness. I am not in a hospital bed with a feeding tube or worse yet, a fatality of this disease—I survived it. I am healthy, and yes—it took time and effort to get to where I am today—but I made it. I do not have regrets—or wish that my childhood could have been different. We are who we are from our experiences but more importantly, our choices. What I have been given from battling this illness is my sense of Self and a sense of living in gratitude. Maintaining a spirit that illuminates value and gratefulness is what keeps me alive. I live in my sixty seconds rather than the sixty seconds of yesterday or tomorrow.

Simplicity, the Heart of Achievement

"The Lord has arranged for us this visit to the earth, but most of us become undesirable guests by considering certain things here as our very own. Forgetting the temporary nature of our stay, we form various attachments: 'my home,' 'my work,' 'my money,' 'my family'. But when our earth-visa expires, all human ties vanish. We are forced to leave behind all we had thought we possessed. The only One that accompanies us everywhere is our Eternal Relative, God."

Paramahansa Yogananda

Thought 61

Learn to live a life of simplicity. Only then can you surround yourself with the physical appetite of the material world. For as the hunger is satisfied, so are the desires. Once you learn to detach yourself from the very essence of what drives you to want, only then can you treasure what you have.

It is when the act of wanting is no longer desired that the Universe provides for us abundantly; with love, family, and material wealth. The action of releasing our desires and needs will not only lesson and cease the worrying, but create a reliance and knowing-ness within that all is provided for. This feeling may puzzle you and you may find yourself not able to understand this new confidence. It is not unusual, for you have just plugged into divine time.

Divinity knows your needs. When you have embraced this, it is then that you have let Divine order not Human order do its job. The timelessness, in which life proceeds, is a consistent rhythm of unseen abundance, only to be recognized by the unspoken voice within each of us.

Appreciation of Life

"As a man is not aware of the fall of a hair, so the Knower of the Self is not aware of the fall of the body in death."

Vedanta

Thought 62

A deep belief in the afterlife can lessen the grief of one's passing. Thoughts of reincarnation is yet another view that can aid and ease the grieving in times of intense sorrow.

To grieve for prolonged periods of time can impede and retard those who have made the transition from the physical plane to another plane of existence. They will be held back by the loved one's thought patterns of grief.

Consequently, we must release their spirit, allowing them to continue their work in the further stages of the Universal evolution. Knowing that they are with us in a different appearance can change our perception of how death is viewed. The form we go back to is the form we were born into—before Time on Earth began.

* * *

This story comes from a dear friend of mine named Kristen. When I first heard of this, I remember thinking that this seemed too unreal, that possibly I had listened to it incorrectly. She has relayed this story more than once to me. Each time I walk away with a more enlightened view that I apply to my own life; particularly the lesson on life's fragility. I hope this story will enlighten you, as it has done for me.

This is Kristen's story:

Growing up, my Dad and I were extremely close. As a kid, I was a tomboy, always hunting and fishing with my father and brother. My father had been a juvenile diabetic since he was a child. I knew he was a diabetic, but I never saw any complications to the disease growing up.

He was insulin dependent, but I never saw him give himself an injection. He very much wanted us to not see that he had this disease.

Thanksgiving of 1990, my parents came up from Illinois to Michigan. We were going to go shopping for a wedding dress and it was hunting season as well. I was planning to go with my Mom, while my Dad was going to go hunting with Chris, my fiancée, and my brother Mike.

I remember sitting in our family room and my Dad saying, *"So are you going to get up early and go pheasant hunting with us"*?

I said, *"Dad...come on, Mom and I are going to shop for a dress. It's kind of a girly thing, I would love to go hunting, but I really can't. The place is open at 9:00 a.m. and we have a lot to do with not a lot of time to do it. If I come hunting with you, you are probably not going to be back until noon, you might even stay the whole day."*

The look of disappointment in his face is one that I cannot forget. It was as if his world had fallen apart. I had never seen him like that. He was always so jovial and happy, you just loved to be around him. When he asked me to go hunting, his tone was solemn. The distress on his face broke my heart. It was as if he felt that this was our last opportunity to do this together. I kept telling him that Mike and Chris were going and that he would have a great time with them. These were the things that I shared with him the most, going for walks, taking the dog out, or hunting and fishing.

The hardest part looking back was that he knew this would be his last time. The next time I noticed something was wrong was at Christmas. My Dad was real quiet, he was moving around cautiously. He was not his normal happy-go-lucky self. I remember the morning we opened presents. I gave my Dad his present and he gave me a hug and started to cry. This was the first time I saw him cry. It bothered me that he was so emotional, because it did not make any sense. I asked him and my mom if everything was fine, it did not even enter my mind that it was the diabetes. I kept thinking it was something at work or that he was getting older and becoming more emotional or maybe he was crying because I was getting married, being his little girl... *I truly didn't know.*

Three weeks before the wedding, my Dad went in for some heart tests, so I drove up from Michigan to be with him. The doctors had told him that he must be at home resting and not go to work. My dad being the way he was did not listen and resumed his work schedule. I decided to go back to Michigan, as he seemed to keep up a good show that everything was great.

The day of both bachelor parties, my brother and I made a conference call to find out about his test results. My dad was silent for a moment.

It was almost as if he could not say the words and then he finally said, *"I am going to be okay."*

He did not say anything more for a few more seconds and then we said, *"well, what did the doctors say, dad, what exactly did they tell you?"*

He replied, *"well, all I have to do is take this medicine and I will be alright*", and he started to cry, but it was more of a choked emotion. It was as if he was grasping for each word. We were very happy at first, because we thought that everything was going to be fine. I asked him why he was crying and he answered, *"because I am just so happy that I am going to be okay."*

My brother then put on this song by Louis B. Armstrong for the three of us to hear. We were all so elated for that moment in time. The song was a milestone in our lives; it was about living life no matter what the consequences were and to the fullest extent. It was about learning to appreciate all the little things and learning to give without really expecting to receive; it was the essence of selfless love. Two weeks prior to the big day, I awoke one night with a terrible dream that my father would die at our wedding. It was a dream I would forever remember.

The night of the rehearsal dinner Chris and I went to pick my parents up. My father was somber. I interpreted this as him being emotional about giving me away. There was another side of me that was concerned, however, for he did not look good. He was moving slowly. When I came to give him a hug, the hug was different. It was a long hug; one that wanted to last an eternity. It was like he was trying to tell me that things were different. He seemed to be fighting his own emotion about wanting to hold me tight, but not wanting me to know.

We were at the church waiting to start the rehearsal procession of the wedding. Chris was at the altar, waiting for my father and I to walk down. When I grabbed my father's arm for him to walk me down, I started walking in my normal fast pace and my dad was walking really, really, slow. He was not one to drag things out, but as he started walking me down the aisle, it was almost as if he wanted it to last, as though, *he wanted to capture tomorrow in today.*

I really feel guilty about that to this day, I remember looking at him and saying, *"Come, dad, we can walk slow tomorrow on the real day."*

When we finished walking down the aisle, my dad was supposed to pass me to Chris. Well, he hesitated: it was almost as if he did not want to sit down. We were standing at the altar and he just stood there for a minute not wanting the moment to end.

I remember looking at him and saying, *"You can sit right here next to mom".*

We all headed toward the restaurant for the rehearsal dinner. My dad was off to my left and I remember sitting there and looking over seeing my parents have a great time. Looking back at the photos, despite my Dad smiling, the smiles were different. They seemed to contain stress and sadness. As the evening progressed, Christopher's mother got up and addressed the audience, saying that it would be nice if they would spend some time reminiscing about Christopher's and my childhood. She asked that each guest bring to the party their experience and memory with one or the other person.

As people were going around the room reminiscing, I would say maybe ten or eleven people had spoken when suddenly I heard Chris's sister stand up and scream, *"Oh my God, someone call 911".*

I did not even have to turn around to look; I just knew it was my father. His face had literally fallen into his plate; and he was bent over.

I remember running down the stairs screaming, *"someone call 911!"*

I ran back upstairs and saw Chris, my brother, and a couple of his friends picking my Dad up and laying him on the floor. I went over, knelt down and saw that his eyes were open but rolling and he seemed to be grasping for breath. I remember screaming to someone to get orange juice, thinking that would help. I remember standing up, rubbing his face, sobbing and saying, *"Dad, please don't go, I love you."*

One of Chris' high school coaches asked us if he should give CPR. At that time we did not know what to do. Looking back, that is what we should have done. It seemed that we sat there forever. Each minute seemed like an hour. We sat and waited and waited. The paramedics got there and worked on my Dad for about twenty minutes trying to resuscitate him, but could not.In the hospital, we were shown a waiting room to sit and wait. A few minutes later, one of the doctors came in and asked us what type of medication my dad was on My mom did not know, she was shaking saying, *"I have no idea... it is back at the hotel."* I was angry with her for not knowing and in a highly emotional state responded, *"How could you not know!"* The doctor asked if anybody could go back to the hotel and find out. The hotel staff could not find it so I turned to Chris and said, *"We are going to the hotel right now"*. I called from the hotel room to inform the doctors of the medication he was taking. We had a glimmer of hope. Upon arriving back at the hospital, twenty minutes later, the doctor walked in and informed my mother that they were sorry; my dad could not be revived. My brother, mom, and I just embraced. The next couple of days were hard, because everything started to make sense. I finally asked my mom, *"Why did dad pass away? He knew, didn't he?"* She said that he did know and when he saw the doctor last, they were not test results he was waiting to get back. He knew the first time he went to see the doctor. The doctors told him that there was nothing they could do, his heart was too weak. Being a diabetic he could not survive a heart transplant, as his heart was weak from the insulin. His chances of receiving a new heart were slim to none, especially for a forty-eight year old diabetic patient. The doctors did not know if he had a day, a week, or a month to live. My dad said to the doctor, *"I don't want you to say anything to anyone, I want this to stay between us and my wife. I want to see my daughter get married, that is all I want to do. I just want to see her get married"*. Looking back, what I know and realize most from my father is that you live your life day by day and you appreciate every moment you have with the ones you love. You don't take anything for granted, ever. There are so many petty things that we let ourselves become upset about. I have realized that in the scheme of things, what really matters is the time you have with the people you love. The little things that get us annoyed are just so insignificant.

What I would give to have just one more day with my dad—I would give anything—because he gave me so much._My dad was one of the most courageous and giving people in the world to have wanted to grant me the happiness of a wedding and make my day so special. It breaks my heart every time I think about it.For a week and a half to two weeks after my dad passed away, I was remembering my dreams continuously. I kept thinking that I was going to have nightmares that I am never going to be able to sleep remembering all the bad things. Ironically, it did not happen that way. I would awake in the middle of the night and be full of tranquility. I would encounter these dreams where I would be walking down a road with my father and we would be talking. I felt as if my entire consciousness was there with him. These dreams felt too real to be only a dream. None of the dreams were sad, they left me with a sense of what he needed to impart to me. I really believe that he was there with me and we were talking and sharing our feelings. I do remember one dream. Although I cannot recall all the specifics, what I do remember was that I was expressing to him something we were going to do together. My dad said, *"well you are going to have to do that alone"*, and I just remember thinking *"but dad you are right here, what do you mean?"* He said, *"but I won't be there—I'll be there for you in mind, but I won't physically be there—you will have to do it alone."*

We had postponed the wedding for a couple of months. I think my dad really tried hard to help us through it. One of the reasons I knew he was there with us was due to the two signs I believe he had shown Chris and me before the wedding. We all went to Henry Ford estate to have pictures taken, Chris and I went down to the river for additional photos. My father had a great passion for the water, outdoors and wildlife. We were standing having our picture taken over looking the water when a salmon jumped. This was April 5th and salmon don't run in April. This huge salmon jumped upstream and was running the river. There was only one, Chris and I both looked at each other with astonishment. I said, *"Oh my God, that's my dad"!* The interesting thing is that the photographer caught a picture of it or no one would have believed us. The second incident occurred when we were walking toward a wooded area that banks all the gardens. Chris and I were looking at the wonderful scenery of the woods, when a red fox started running toward us. Foxes are very sly and shy: you do not see them and especially not in developed areas such as Dearborn, Michigan. They are nocturnal and do not show themselves in the light. There must have been thirty or forty people coming with us for pictures and all quite loud. The noise did not deter the fox, as it kept running through the woods towards us. It stopped barely a few feet away, looked at us with a long pause and trotted away. Things like that are not so common. The photographer got a picture of that as well. It was then that I knew my father was trying to let me know that he was with Chris and me. My heart was filled with his love, as he shared our day from his world. About two months after my dad had passed away, Chris and I bought a small home. It was a beautiful spring day in May. I remember going and sitting on the bathroom floor, remembering my father. Chris walked in and sat beside me. The window was opened and it was a still night. It was one of those nights where a breeze could not be found. Chris asked me what I was thinking about, I said, *"you know what I am thinking about"*. He said, *"you're thinking about your dad"*, and I said *"yeah"*. I started reminiscing about some of the things dad and I used to do. I was crying and laughing simultaneously, speaking about some of the funny things we did together. The second I started to laugh, the wind chimes hanging from our porch went off. It was incredibly loud. There was not a breeze anywhere. We were sitting right beside the window where we could see the porch and the chimes. I just looked at Chris and said *"Oh my God, that's dad!"* We both knew he was here. It was as if he was conveying in his own way what a good story that was. The one thing I look back on that I really remember the most about my dad, was that he always lived for the moment. One of the biggest things I have learned is that no matter how great a relationship you have or do not have with your parents, you need to appreciate the time left with them. We never know when God will. They are your family and they do love you in their own way. We are all dealt different cards in life. We need to handle whatever cards we have in the best way we know how.

Thought 63

When one has transcended from the physical plane to the next plane of existence, prayers that are sent are of utmost significance.

These prayers when received are similar to rays of light absorbed by the loved ones who have departed from the earth plane. It aids in their transition and helps them adjust to a new, but familiar environment. The impact that our thoughts create and manifest for ourselves and for others is substantial.

When spirit enters the next plane, their awareness becomes more fine-tuned than that of the earth plane. They are able to see a bigger, possibly more complete picture as their comprehension sharpens and consciousness heightens. The last thing they would want to see or feel from the ones who are left behind, are thoughts of guilt, anger, blame, or intense anguish. This does not help their adjustment or transition and can subsequently hinder their own development.

There is a master plan, although at times difficult to fathom as events sometimes do not turn out the way we intend for them to.

However, from time to time the greater the impact, the more intensified the learning. Leaving us to ponder that every occurrence in our lives is about growth. And as the seasons enfold into each other, so does the soul of life, as spirit carries on.

Thought 64

As descent of darkness deepens and one more day bids us good-bye, observe the silhouette of darkness that spirals upon the light. Do not wait for a distant tomorrow if something can be voiced in the here and now.

Once in a while, pride and ego can leave us with a sense of regret and questions of "what if". However, if we learn to live in present time and not in the presence of fear, pride, or anger, we become a part of time, which is a component of the Universe.

We will discover that instead of running around Time, we will seize the flood of time. Leading us to verbalize the things that need to be said and aiding us in completing the things that need to be done. This is the core of living in the living moment.

* * *

This story comes from a friend who has this to say on gratefulness, recognition and life.

This is Dawn's story:

Grabbing the moment, opening our hearts, speaking our minds, and asking the questions we need to ask to the people in our lives is what appreciation means to me. My grandmother passed away in September 1998. She was a second mother to me because she raised me for a good part of my growing years. In my deepest core, I never really believed that she could die in spite of the fact that I had learnt about death at a young age with the passing of my father. Death was always something real; I had always been keenly aware that the people I love could be gone tomorrow. However, at some very deep level, she was the one person that I didn't believe could leave. She was a constant in my life, not an easy person by any stretch, but always there for me. Over the last couple of years, she was diagnosed with Huntington's disease. In the last two to three years of her life, the disease progressed rapidly. Her mind was sharp till the end, but she would not always be present as she often drifted into another realm. For fourteen years, my grandmother was the number one real estate broker in the state of Massachusetts. Everywhere I went, people knew her. People adored her. She was not like any real estate broker today. She remembered birthdays, Christenings, and was always so involved in her customer's lives. The fact that she became so different from who she used to be was a dramatic change for all of us. Living so far away, I would go home once or twice a year to see her. What I realize now was that I was slowly closing my eyes to her, as it was too painful to watch her this way. When I visited my grandparents I would visit with my grandfather. Here is where I would spend valuable time, while I had superficial time with my grandmother. I would always squeeze a small visit with her, but every time it got too close, I would back off. On some grievous level, it hurt too much. In the spring of 1998, it began to occur to me that she might not be around forever. I started to feel that I had let too much time go by. I realized she was not really there for me anymore as she had been and that I needed to have some closure and meaningful time with her. I decided to go home by myself, without my children and husband. What expedited this decision was that she was suddenly moved to a nursing home. This was something she always said she would never do. I knew that if it had come this far, I had been blind for too long. I made plans to go to Cape Cod and see her. Before I went, all my relatives kept telling me that I was wasting my time and money going there. She was not going to talk with me and that I was not going to get anything out of it. They told me not get my hopes up and think that I will have some meaningful time with her. They said that they could barely spend ten minutes with her, as all she does is stare off into space.

Well, I did go to see her, and for the first time in five years—I really *saw* her. This opening began the acknowledgement on both our parts of life's fragility. Thus, I felt a strong need to verbalize some of the things that I always wanted to say. She had been a very complicated person and our family was quite dysfunctional growing up, leaving some very painful events in our history that she was central to. I needed to voice certain things that might be hurtful. I felt that I needed to be really honest with her, so that the two of us could connect. I talked with her and addressed it very openly. I said to her, *"it is really hard to see you like this, you don't look anything like I have always seen you. You look very frail"*.Many things I said would have people gasping and remarking about the inappropriateness, especially to someone in her condition. However, my grandmother was the kind of person who told you what she thought. It was what she had passed on to me. She taught me to speak my mind and to express my anger as well as my love. I felt that in her darker days, she needed that from me. She did not need me to play a game that was not real. She did not need for me to pretend that the nursing home was wonderful and that she looked beautiful, so I didn't. I told her that I had been turning my back on her for three years, as I couldn't face the changes in her. I made this trip so as to not turn my back anymore. I think I was the only person who was honest about where things had gotten to. Everyone else was trying to convince her how well she was doing and where she was was a beautiful place to live. Well, she wasn't doing well. Although it was a decent place, it was not the kind of place she wanted to end her life. At the nursing home, I wanted to take her out for a walk. It was a beautiful spring day and she had not left her room since she took residence, which was about a month. She refused, but I pushed the wheelchair out the door and stroked her hair as we began to really speak. I told her how much I was going to miss her when she was gone. I told her how much I had learnt from her and how much she meant to me in my life. I wanted to make sure nothing was left unsaid, pertinent or not. In the end, she loved the walk so much, that from that day, she demanded to be taken out everyday. At one point during my stay there, I was sitting in her room and looking into her eyes. I started telling her how much I loved her and how I missed her. I said, *"I just miss who you were, I miss being able to talk with you".* I started to cry, as she just stared blankly at me. The Huntington's disease has that effect. It's a very vulnerable thing to be crying and having someone just sit there. I leaned over and hugged her and she just sat there. I was sobbing into her neck saying, *" Grandma, I need a hug so badly right now, I need you to hold me, I miss that more than anything".* As I was hugging her, she pulled the strength together and put her arms around me and held me. She kept holding and patting my back in a soothing way. It was at that moment that I realized that she had heard everything I had said. It was then that we really connected and it was then that I knew that she knew what she was going through. In August, I went to see her again, but this time with my children and we had a wonderful visit. Two weeks later, I received the most devastating call; my mother informed me that my grandmother had passed on the night before. I totally was unprepared. As much as I intellectually thought it through, it left me unprepared.

I did my grandmother's eulogy and picked her burial site for cremation, but when I came home I was left with this horrible emptiness. Over the weeks, when I began to come to terms with her passing, what I realized was that I was so grateful to have taken that time to really talk with her and really listen to her. I was so grateful for the time we shared where I told her what I really needed to say…the good and the bad. It was not so important that I voice to her that I loved her, for she knew that. When someone is taken from us— sometimes people feel regrets about not telling the person that they loved them. Through my eyes, it shouldn't matter whether one voices it that particular day, the loved one can feel and know that the love was always there, even if it was not verbalized. There are other things that we may need to say that are important for who we are. For me, it was critical to say to her that there were times in my life that she really hurt me but what I really learned is that she also loved me so much that the hurt did not matter as much as the love did. To say those things was a healing process for me, but I think it was good for her as well. I treated her like her old self. She needed that, she did not want to be treated like an invalid or a person trapped in a body with no mind. I have come away from this experience feeling that it is especially important to say to the people we love not just that we love them, but what they really mean to us in all forms. When my grandmother was gone, I did not feel like there was anything I did not get to say. I think we all wish we had more time. Whenever you love someone, there is never a good time to lose them. There always could have been more things to say. Nevertheless, I said what I felt in my heart, I said what I knew in my soul. These were the most important things for me and for us. It was in these moments that *I heard her and she heard me.*

Liberation of the Soul

"Liberation or attainment of perfection is a condition experienced by the mind; liberation is only for the mind because the mind alone was in bondage."

Swami Chinmayananda

Thought 65

When we feel that someone has destroyed or violated our inner being, when we feel hurt towards another, remember humankind needs to embrace the realization that:

We are not the body-we are the Soul.

We are not the mind-we are the Absolute.

We are not flesh, intellect, nor vitals-we are simply Spirit, ethereal in nature.

With that understanding we must come to know that freewill, liberation and enlightenment—we are.

Our heads must be held high with pride, dignity, and grace, knowing that no person can occupy another's Consciousness. Although they may grasp for it, they have yet to arrest its esprit. Like a butterfly evading its capture, our essence can only be seized when the Self is yet to be discovered.

If, within the Self, you can embrace this knowledge with clarity—you have engaged onto the path of enlightenment.

* * *

This story comes from a woman named Teresa who, through her story, has shown me what liberation truly means.

This is Teresa's story:

It is interesting how when some of the very worst things happen to you, they turn out to be the very things that define you. A few years ago when I was twenty-eight, I started having flashbacks of things that happened to me as a child. I always knew that I was different and that there was something that kept me apart and very separate from other children. This continued as I went to high school. I felt alone being around a bunch of people. It never really made any sense to me as to why I felt so disconnected from everything, total disconnection. I did not feel connected to anything.

My mother had me as a single parent and when I was about two years old, she started dating a man, which she ended up marrying. He subsequently adopted me and I took his name. What I started to remember was that he abused me in a sexual way while I grew up. It wasn't so much the part about the abuse that was traumatic; it was letting myself remember and accept that it did happen and trying to find my connection. That is why I felt so disconnected and isolated, that is why I did not feel like others and always felt a sense of floating. The abuse started from about age four or five and lasted till I was eleven. I did not have anyone to relate the experience to and in my own little world as a child I was not even aware what was happening to me was bad, good or abnormal.

While the abuse was going on, I would disassociate. I would bite my nails, leave my body or I would live inside the stories of my mind while it was going on. Literally, that is what I had to do in order to live through it. I had to separate the abuse from the real world I was living in. It was too chaotic for it all to be going on in the same place. I did most of my disassociation through books; I would read fifteen to twenty paperbacks a week. I lived in my room. I would only come out to eat and sometimes watch television with my family. Other then that, I would lock my door and read or listen to records.

As I got older into my teens, the abuse became more physical. All I would do from the age of fourteen to seventeen is concentrate on getting out. When I graduated from high school, I worked hard to make money that summer so that I could leave for college. I left in August and thought I was free. Soon enough time would relay to me how imprisoned I truly was. However, only my physical being was free from being confined to a place that I hated, but my inner core was not, as I had all this pent up emotion inside of me.

The college years were a blur to me, as I was a heavy drinker. I would drink not because I liked to drink, but to numb the pain. As I got older, I had to come up with some new and creative ways to block it out. When you are a child, the brain is equipped with some wonderful mechanisms where children can very easily compartmentalize and pretend it did not happen; then literally never remember it again if they choose not too. At that time of course, I did not understand that this was the reason for my drinking. I would just drink until I blacked out. I also put on weight, which was another barrier; only it was a physical one.

I went into therapy in January 1995, initially, because my marriage was in trouble. I had an incredible therapist who took me down a path where she helped me understand that no matter what had happened to me, I was still pure and good. I had a good soul and a good heart. Although terrible things had happened to me, those things did not define who I was. Who I was, was much greater and came from a very different place than where all the pain came from.She re-parented me. I did not have a good mother and I obviously did not have a good father. Due to my occupation as a therapist and because of my understanding of therapy from my background and degree, we were able to do what one would consider alternative therapy. She specifically worked with visual imagery and meditation. We did a lot of chakra work. I would tell her that I was feeling sick in a certain area and she would ask me to point the area out to her. We would then deal with that specific chakra and understand why I am hurting there and why I feel sick. She was very good at defining each Chakra and the emotional biography behind it. To this day, when I feel unbalanced I ask myself where do I feel bad, as that tells me right away what is going on within me. If it is in the stomach area, which is the second chakra, then I am aware that my identity is affected and I am feeling threatened in some way. My very being is feeling that something is not right and that I need to protect it. If it is in my neck and shoulders, the fifth chakra, then I know that I am probably carrying way too much. I have over maximized myself, carrying more than I need. Another area where I would experience pain was my heart, which is the fourth chakra. I would get incredible chest pains, which were agonizing. She taught me what these pains meant and how they related to my emotions and cell tissue. She was very in tuned to what part of you was hurting and what you were feeling and remembering. Any part of the body would be referred back to the chakras and what feelings emanated from that. She would always make me reference it back to another time in my life when I felt that way before. This was the key to unlocking everything. By her doing this consistently, it became my way of thinking and living. If I felt bad, I would proceed one step further and ask myself to think when was there a time that I felt like this before. Consequently, my subconscious would give me the answer. Due to the nature of the trauma I had been through, I do not believe I would have been well today if the therapy were not through some type of alternative method; like the Chakra system my therapist incorporated. I eliminated relationships that were based on the wrong boundaries and concepts that I had learnt as a child; this is where my marriage came into play. I loved my husband, but it was not a husband and wife relationship; he had been my best friend for a number of years. I felt trapped in a marriage, the same way I was trapped at home when I was a child. I was making due, accepting what was given to me and making the best of it. Living all those years making the best of it and finally healing, I realized that I did not have to make the best of it any more: *I can have what I want.* I can reach for what I need, and it is really O.K. I truly felt that I was elevating to my sense of *Oneness* and completion and better able to see with my third eye the things I needed to fulfill in this lifetime.I am happier than I have ever been in my life. I have become disentangled from my past. I would like to say it was the therapy, but the therapy was a stepping-stone to teaching me how to see. What I implement now, which I never did before, is listen to the inner me. I give ear to what my body, mind, and spirit are conveying to me. This is mainly done around the third Chakra in the Solar Plexus area; this is the defining Chakra for that. It transmits to me everything I need to know. If I encounter somebody who may not be good or right for me, my stomach will tell me. I will feel a physical pull toward that person if I feel right about them. On the other hand, if I feel that this is not a good person, I will feel a clamping or a pinch.I now view life as a journey. I shifted from seeing my life with horror to understanding that I am the person I am today due to the experiences that occurred in my life. I am going to be thirty-one years old and I feel like I am finally living. I am not living through others or for others, I am living for me. Some people who have had the childhood trauma that I experienced have a hard time evolving beyond it, which is one of the reasons we did the alternative Eastern approach. I did not just want to accept this and live with it; I wanted to go past it. I wanted my body, mind, and spirit to move beyond it. I needed to let this go.I used to say that my soul was broken and that my soul would never heal, but it has healed. Yes, I do have a scar, but it is not a scar from being wounded, it is a scar that I wear proudly because to me it signifies a battle that I have won. This scar reminds me that our soul has the ability to heal and that one can carry on no matter what happens. I do not believe that we should allow what happens to us define who we are in a negative sense, to the effect that I am an incest survivor. If someone walked up to me and told me that they were an incest survivor, I would be inclined to say, *"so what-yes, you are and good for you for surviving, but what are you now doing with your life"*. I do not walk around and identify myself as an incest survivor; that is a very small piece of who I am. Although at some point, it seemed to be a very big part of me. The older I get and as the months go by, it seems to get tinier and tinier. I do not want to define myself by my pain or my past. I feel that putting pain in perspective is one of the most difficult tasks all of us have, but we need to embrace our pain and let it go. People who are not as aware or open tend to wait for the big miracle that will change their life. I have come to realize that we must be aware of life's small subtleties; in life it is the small stuff that tends to be the things that are most significant. That is why they are inclined to get overlooked so many times. If there is any thing that I can impart to another, is to love your whole Self, your physical, your mental, your pain, your past, and your spirit. When you learn how to love your whole Self, the Universe will surround you with people who also love the whole Self that resides within you.

Thought 66

To rape is to take away what was never yours. Rape can come not only in the physical sense, but also as an emotional guise. All of us have been willing victims or perpetrators of emotional rape at some point in our lives.

When we take away from another by lashing out or laughing at someone's expense, we have taken. When we force our views upon others; whether it is on religion, raising a family. etc., we have taken. When we argue or fight with others, we take and are being taken from. *Both can be seen as victims and perpetrators.*

For the Love of Our Ego

"The ego and the Self dwell as intimate friends in the same body,
like two golden birds perched in the same tree,
The ego eats the sweet and the sour fruits of the tree,
While the Self looks on detached.
For as long as you identify with the ego,
You will feel joy and sorrow.
But if you know you are the Self, the Lord of Life,
You will be free from suffering;
The supreme source of love.
You will transcend duality
And live in a state of Oneness."

Mundaka Upanishad

Thought 67

We have all been blessed with an ego—and to some extent an ego is needed to carry out some of God's work. However, a person graced with an over abundance is immersed in the mind of Self-gratification. They prefer to ***be-out***, rather than ***be-in***. Most of their conversations relate back to their experiences. They gather information, judgment, and lack any real concentrated effort in listening to the other person. By learning to listen without interruption, one forms the first step in becoming balanced.

Listening is like meditation. Think how difficult it is to keep other thoughts from intruding when you meditate. Subsequently, one gently guides those thoughts away, while remaining centered on the breathing and mantra (sacred verse or name of God). The same principle should be applied to listening. When your mind starts to wander, gently focus its attention back to the one who is speaking.

Thought 68

When we incarnate into our bodies, we attain a degree of egoism. It is part of our human makeup. However, if the ego is the dominating trait of our personality, this results in the Self becoming separated from its Absolute, its Source—the Atman (soul). In this dimension, the foundation is constructed on wants and desires of the physical plane.

An egoist is a person where his/hers perimeters have been built on vulnerability. These walls are fragile and can be broken quickly. It is not hard to decipher weakness in them, however hard they may camouflage it. It permeates through their spirit and language. The need to implement the "I" in a conversation is one example.

They are somewhat uncomfortable around others, although one would think otherwise. This is why most of their conversation relates back to them. They lack a deep sense of relating to another by virtue of not being able to relate to their Self. The ego, unlike our consciousness, is built solely on the exoteric world— our outer reality. The inner work has never existed within them. For this reason, being plugged into external circuits, instead of internal ones, is a safer route to follow.

Therein lies a painless path.

The Truth is Within...

"Truth is One and the learned call it by many names."
Rig Veda

Thought 69

How can one find truth? Wisdom emerges from inner inquiry—dwelling on the *with-in.* It is the basic crux that separates intuition from reasoning. Wisdom goes beyond collective truth. It reaches into individual truth that lays dormant until awakened by an expansion of our Consciousness that no longer divides, but unites.

Truth is unchanging and varies from individual to individual. The truth of your soul is different from the truth in mine. That is how each one of us ascertains our inner enlightenment and karma.

* * *

This story comes from a woman named Thelma whom I met at a baby shower for a mutual friend of ours.

This is Thelma's story:

The year was 1967, I was fourteen years of age and diagnosed with a disease called Guillain Barre. It is a disease that begins by numbing your body— feet first, and works its way upward toward the respiratory system. Due to the affects the disease had on my respiratory system, I was on a respirator for six to eight weeks. During my stay at the hospital, which was from September 1967 to March 1968, I found myself in and out of consciousness.

At that time, three exceptional occurrences took place while I lay in bed. One of the three experiences came to pass when I was fully conscious and aware of my surroundings. I was lying in my bed when I felt a warm hand on my forehead. I would then actually feel an undergoing of healing throughout my body. I could feel this warm energy stream into me. When I would open my eyes, the feeling would disappear, but when I kept them closed, I would again feel this energetic warmth. It was quite odd.

The second instance occurred when I was pronounced clinically dead. My aunt who was with me for most of my stay, recalls the doctors telling her that they had brought me back to life. I do not remember ever being dead, as I was already going on what I have labeled *my journey*. I awoke to a place where it was warm and bright. If you could imagine the most brilliant, sunniest day here on earth, you would have some idea of what I encountered. I felt the most indescribable peace in this place. I cannot even tell you what I experienced because there are no words suitable in this language to give you an accurate picture. There was no pain here. I felt that I could run and play like a normal fourteen year old child usually does. Something I had not experienced since I had become sick and something I knew I could not do if I was back at the hospital in my earthly body.

The last experience I encountered was a vision. I saw at the foot of my bed, a man smiling in a white gown. You could see through this vision. His hands were opened and in his palms I noticed a hole through each. On his head lay a crown of thorns and his hair was long, coarse, and flowing. His skin color was neither white nor black but was golden bronze. His eyes were the color of the Caribbean Sea, it was an astonishing blue-green. It was in his eyes that you could see forever. It was in his eyes that you felt that you were looking literally into eternity. They were never ending.

Many people of other faiths can call this vision by another name, but to me this man was Jesus. When I was finally able to tell others what I had seen, many discounted my story. At the church I had attended, many of its members and some of my friends said that it was impossible to feel healing hands, or to see Jesus. Their rationale was that no one has seen Jesus, meaning they had not, so their conclusion was that I was hallucinating and dreaming.

It has been thirty-one years since the hospital incident. I believe to this day what I witnessed was a vision. My eyes saw this apparition as Jesus, I have no doubt that he touched and healed me during my stay at the hospital. Depending on your faith, you may see it differently in your belief system. However, whether this vision was Jesus or not, more importantly, it was a vision of LOVE to me. I am a healthcare aide and when I recount my journey to some of my patients, many have recalled similar incidents. They have not seen Jesus, but have gone through a tunnel of light, where they did not want to come back. In my experience, it was like going to sleep and waking up in a place where you want to be, a place with indefinable peace and where pain, suffering, and sorrow do not reign. I look forward to going back home, but for now I live my life the best way I know how each day. I do not live to go back, I live to be the best person I can with the time I have left. I know that when my time draws near, death will only be a rebirth.

What I have taken from this experience is that inner truth is very individual. Who are we to decide what another person's truth may be? I believe in what I saw. There are those who believe in what I have experienced and there are those who discount it; I am fine with both. I believe that each one of us holds our own truth within. I believe that there is only one God worshipped across the world in many forms, each with their own truth. I have come to realize through this experience that there is truth in each one of us, no matter who we are or what we believe in. God loves all of us. If I have inspired one person from my experience, I know that I have done my job.

Thought 70

Have an open mind to 'different' literature! Make an attempt to broaden the seeds of development. Although, you may find yourself not understanding a piece of work, give your Self time as your consciousness undertakes and assimilates this new knowledge. Periodically, we need to expand our horizons by going beyond the viewpoints of others, by keeping in mind that not all great minds think alike!

There have been many noteworthy works of creation dismissed by adept authority only to be adored by thousands later. *The Celestine Prophecy* is but one example. Do not rely on the voices of others to make your decision. Remember, they are only opinions based on their reality.

Moreover, experts may be bound by their own borders. Often times they tend to place too much 'critical thought' on an undertaking. This inclination may block their cognizance in regards to the spiritual essence of the piece.

The Power in Prayer

"Even as rivers spring from different sources,
Yet mingle in the ocean,
So all the Vedas, all Scriptures, all Truth, though of diverse origin,Come home to thee!"

Swami Prabhavananda

Thought 71

Prayers are conversations with God. We must recognize that All prayers are heard the instant they are thought. Sometimes, when we pray for the greatest burden to be removed, the answer comes in the strength to carry it out—*producing a blessing.* From time to time, our greatest desire can be our worst burden.

When we pray for things that we need or would like to receive; we must first ask of ourselves, how have we helped in answering another person's prayer? God filters through various channels and one of those forms is the human race.

Before we ask God to ease our pain—we must ask God what pain can we ease from another?

* * *

This story represents the power of prayer of all faiths.

This is Ramesh's story:

In March 1999, my daughter-in-law Sonya had a slight temperature and some coughing. She was finishing her eighth month of pregnancy—a pregnancy she had long anticipated through several years of trying and fertility medication. Her due date was towards the end of April. On the 6th of April she was taken to the hospital around 8:00 a.m., where she delivered normally two hours later a baby boy. However, it was after the delivery that the problems began. She could not stop bleeding; they had transfused 26 pints of blood into her. A normal human body has five pints of blood and Sonya took nearly six peoples' blood.

She stayed in the ICU for about a month and half and then she went back home. She seemed fine in the ensuing months that followed. On the 12th of August, my son called me saying that he took Sonya to the hospital, as she was having tremendous pain in her abdomen and was vomiting continuously. My wife and I planned to go that day but my son had told us to wait as her condition was up and down. The next day, which was Saturday, my son called and said that she seemed fine. She was walking around her room and that they would probably leave the hospital by Saturday evening.

We received a call Saturday night at 11:30 p.m. from my son Neil saying that Sonya slipped into a coma and was taken for emergency surgery. That night we called our friend Dr. Ratan for advice. He said he would contact Sonya's doctor and see if it was ok to discuss her case with him. The next morning my wife and I flew to Minneapolis. When we arrived, the diagnosis that was given on her condition was Adult Respiratory Distress Syndrome. What had happened was that her small intestine was wrapped around the main artery, which supplies blood to the intestine—and twelve inches of the intestine was dead. The enzyme or bacteria from that intestine was mixed into the blood and went straight into the lungs. Her lungs were completely full from the bacteria, which is why she went into a coma.

When they did her surgery, they removed twelve inches of her intestine. Medically speaking, it is called gangrene of the bowel. However, she remained in a coma and was hooked onto a respirator. A respirator normally breathes for a person maximum 60-64% beats per minute, more then 64% becomes very dangerous, as the lungs or heart could collapse. She had her surgery on the 14th of August and on the 19th she took a turn for the worse. The respirator began breathing about 80-84% for her. Dr. Ratan, our family friend and physician, made the decision to fly to Minneapolis. A meeting with all of Sonya's physicians was planned for Sunday afternoon, so Dr. Ratan and Dr. Patel, another family friend, flew on Sunday morning. The Radiologist, Pulmonist, Cardiologist, Sonya's surgeon, and the Infection Control physician were present along with Drs. Ratan and Patel.

When the meeting was over, Dr. Ratan gave me the indication that Sonya would be here only for the next couple of days. Part of what he was trying to convey to me was to be prepared to give strength to the family. Dr. Patel called his wife in and asked her to organize a community puja (prayer ceremony) to be done immediately at the temple. Whoever could attend would be welcomed. The puja (prayer ceremony) was scheduled for 8:00 p.m. Monday night. Mrs. Ratan requested we hold a prayer session in the hospital room at the same time, which would be 7:00 p.m. our time. We were praying daily, but this was the first organized prayer chain.

That same day, Dr. Ratan suggested to the Pulmonary Specialist that perhaps Sonya should lie on her stomach. The Pulmonary specialist said he had heard that sometimes it does make a difference. However, since Sonya had a tracheotomy, any sudden moves could be fatal if the tube was moved and oxygen was not being supplied to the brain within a four-minute span. On that account, changing her position from her back to the stomach had to be done carefully. Doctors were reluctant, but decided to go ahead and do it for one hour. Dr. Ratan said that he would take responsibility and convince the family. They turned her for one hour and soon could see her respirator coming down from 87 beats per minute to 70 beats per minute. They decided to continue this for three hours altogether on Sunday.

In the meantime, my daughter and son-in-law in Washington, along with their friends, also took part in organizing the scheduled prayer time for Monday night. Similarly, another daughter in New York held a scheduled prayer session at her house. The same thing transpired in San Francisco, where Sonya's brother lived, for 5:00 p.m. on Monday. We called relatives in India and they were going to hold it at 6:00 a.m. their time Tuesday morning. Whomever we knew, we called and asked if they could pray at this particular hour on Monday night.

On Monday at 6:30 p.m. Minneapolis time she was turned over on her stomach. Sonya's respirator was breathing for her at 87% and her pulse rate had accelerated to 179. During the prayer session, the respirator came down to 64%, which is a normal reading if it reads between 62-64%. Her pulse rate came down to 126. After the prayer session was over, many of the nurses and doctors came to us and said that they had asked their family members to prayer that hour in their home, church, synagogue, mosque, and temple. The surgeon who performed surgery on Sonya asked our permission if his daughter and family could organize a session at their church for that hour. We said yes, as we believe that it does not matter which version of God one prays to, as all paths in our scriptures lead to ONE.

After Monday, her respiration never went higher then 66 beats per minute and her pulse came down slowly, although still in a coma. She remained in a coma state for about two and a half months with prayers being continuous. Medical personnel who were Christian brought candles from their churches. Those who were Hindu came with vibuthi (holy ash) from the temples and those of the Jewish faith brought holy water from the synagogue. Some community members started calling up the temples in India, Hawaii, Pittsburgh, and New York where vibuthi (holy ash) was sent to be applied to her forehead everyday.

By the end of September, my wife, Dr. Ratan's daughter and I flew to Minneapolis to see Sonya. Kerin began to speak saying, *"Sonya, I am Kerin, and I am here."*

No sooner did those words come out of Kerin's mouth when Sonya opened her eyes and gave her a smile. My son and I left the room so Sonya and Kerin could continue to converse as we did not want to interrupt this precious moment. From that moment onwards, things went uphill. She left ICU in the beginning of October and by the 15th of October she began a complete rehabilitation. She began to relearn the smallest of movements from the fingers to her toes, to chewing and swallowing. We did not know how much damage had taken place and if it was temporary or permanent. They did quite a few tests on her and there was some harm to the lungs and the heart, but the brain, liver and urinary tract were doing well. We did not care how much time it took as long she recovered completely. With God's grace and with everyone's prayers and blessings, her recovery went smoothly.

She came home around the 20th of October and stayed in Minneapolis for one week. The following Saturday we flew her to our home in Michigan. Since then she has been recovering and getting reacquainted with her baby in our home. I have learned two things from this experience with my daughter-in-law: never lose faith in God and to be surrounded by good friends. This is the sum and substance of life, to give without motive and to be able to receive when help is being offered.

Many physicians have asked my daughter-in-law what should they tell others from her experience.

This is what she said, " *Petty things in life don't matter to me anymore. Every morning when I awake I am happy that I can open my eyes and see the sun outside. I am happy with what I have. There was a strong possibility that I could have lost my voice or the use of my arms or legs. I am grateful to have regained my body back and have the ability to hold my son and play with him daily.*

Whatever you want to do, you should do it at that time. If you feel that you made a mistake, say you're sorry to that person at that minute. When I was taken away for surgery, I knew there might be a chance I may not come back. I held my sister and husband's hand and I told them to take care of my son. I voiced to my husband to remarry and told both of them that I loved them dearly. When they were taking me on the stretcher, so many thoughts went through my mind on what I could have said to my husband, mother, sister, father-in-law, etc.

If I could impart something of what I have grasped from all of this, it is not to hold thoughts in your mind because you may never get a second chance to say them. If you are unhappy about something voice it. If you love someone say it, because you don't want to take these emotions with you. There were so many things that I wanted to say to my husband as I was taken away that I did not get a chance to voice. Many times we don't have the time once our time nears. We need to finish our unfinished business by living in the moment."

Thought 72

What makes one prayer go unanswered as another is fulfilled? Many aspects go into the process of unanswered prayers: timing, karma, grace, and personal effort. But sometimes it is lessons yet to be learned. If somehow we have not learned from a circumstance, it would only be repeated, hence, leaving us on an endless cycle.

Past and present karma play a significant role in teaching the lessons that we must learn in order to move ahead. Answers to prayers are received when the time is right. All prayers are heard the instant they are formed and all prayers are eventually fulfilled—while some remain blessings in disguise.

* * *

This story came from a friend named Jo-k who shared this story about answered prayers and blessings in disguise.

This is Jo-k's story:

My husband Mike and I rented a Tahoe for the weekend. This was the Sunday before Thanksgiving 1997. Mike was going to go get some gas, as we had to fill it up before giving it back that Monday. It was a chilly night about 10:00 p.m., so Mike decided to warm the car up. As the car was warming up, he had come back inside to get some money. As he walked through the front door he turned around to see that our Tahoe was going down the road. Mike started screaming, *"Our car is being stolen!"*

He quickly jumped into our other car and chased the Tahoe down the street. I can't even tell you how long he was following it, as both cars went down different streets. Luckily, the Tahoe stopped as a train was coming across the tracks. At that moment, Mike jumped out of his car and was fighting to get into the front seat of the Tahoe. He then jumped onto the Tahoe's front hood. By that time, the train had passed and the kid accelerated the vehicle forward. Mike had fallen off the car and onto the ground where the Tahoe ran over his leg. The driver did not get very far; he ended up ditching the vehicle and running, while Mike hobbled to a house for help. The police caught the teenager a few hours later. We later found out that it was a fourteen-year old boy who lived with his grandmother and who had a record of being in and out of trouble frequently. The story he gave the police was that my husband was buying drugs from him and that he did not take off with the car. It then went through the court system.

When he came home that day, my first thought was, "oh, my God, he cannot work, what are we going to do"? I really felt awful to think this, but we were barely making ends meet. I was five months pregnant, working as a social worker and taking night classes for a teaching degree, while Mike worked for a heating and cooling company. We were living paycheck to paycheck, which is typical of couples our age.

We went to the emergency room and found out that the leg was broken. Since this did not happen at work, I started thinking that Mike might not going to be compensated for lost wages. My mind raced in a panic as I thought we would have to file for bankruptcy. We, like most couples, had house payments, car payments, school, and getting ready for our new baby. I kept thinking that it would not be as bad if I were not pregnant, that I could probably waitress at night and on weekends to compensate for his income, however, being five months pregnant would be difficult. I sat in the emergency room feeling a little sorry for myself and thinking, *"why me God—why us? Don't we have enough bad luck as it is?"* I always thought that we had bad luck and some would remark thinking that way brings it on, but I could not help myself at that moment. I thought our life was over financially. I stayed in the emergency room overnight and was praying for any small miracle to manifest. I went to work the following morning and took my exam that evening at school. Mike was ordered by his physician to stay off his leg.

We called the car insurance company, as they needed to have the car towed and checked due to it being stolen. While conversing on the phone with the agent, he informed us that our policy did cover lost wages. He said that Mike was a pedestrian and in that situation our insurance will cover it. I could not believe what I was hearing. I said to Mike, *"Oh my Lord, thank you God"*. The insurance ended giving us 100% of Mike's wages, but we never thought he would be off for more then a couple of weeks. We later found out that there was more ligament damage and he was off longer than expected. The baby was born in March and we had thought that Mike would be back to work soon after. My next worry was finding a babysitter and the fears that come with sending your newborn baby off to be taken care of by a stranger. Mike's leg got worse and he ended up having another surgery scheduled for April. The surgery did not take well and incurred additional problems. The good thing that came out of all this mess is that he has been able to stay home with our son Jacoband still earn money. We could not have wished for anything better.

Mike has never really been around kids, so in the beginning I was quite worried about what type of caretaker he would be to Jacob. From the start, Mike was wonderful. I could not have asked for a better person to take care of our son. I sometimes wonder if I could have been that gentle and patient, as Mike has been to Jacob. He is with him constantly, one on one. Mike bestows onto Jacob his complete and undivided attention. When I come home from work and start to do things with the baby, Mike will tell me what Jacob likes best. Sometimes he will come over and show me which way Jacob likes to be held or what speed he prefers best in the motorized swing, or which food is best for the time of day.

My husband has totally taken on the maternal role. Some days he will turn to me and say *"just look at him"*, and I will say, *"I am looking"*, and he would say, *"No... just look at him... isn't he the most beautiful thing, I love him so much—you don't know how much I love him".* He came to my work with Jacob once and sat with one of my co-workers and said, *" Brenda, just look at him"*, and Brenda said, *" yes, he is cute",* and then Mike said, *"Isn't he just—beautiful"*.I now come home to dinner on the table, a house cleaned, and the baby's laundry folded and put away. Mike is a complete Mr. Mom.

The other day he turned to me as I lay on the bed studying and said, *"if you would hang up at least one piece of clothing from the basket it would be emptied in no time."*

I laughed and thought to myself what a role reversal! Normally that would have been me saying that to him!

I know this sounds sexist, but I never thought a man could take on such a motherly role, especially my husband. It is so beautiful to watch them interact with each other. Many men either do not have the time for their kids or don't take the time. I am just so thankful to God that Mike was able to stay home with Jacob and receive the type of bonding that usually occurs between mother and child.I had no faith that it would have worked out so beautifully. I was too busy thinking what bad luck we had. I would have never thought in a million years that this situation would have ended up so positive. This was a blessing in disguise for our family. Jacob has been able to stay home with Mike, instead of being a forty-hour plus daycare baby.

We appreciate each other's roles, because we stepped into each other's roles. He says to me, he does not know how I do it—going to work and school full time. I say to him if the house were left up to me it would look like a tornado. He accomplishes so much more than I could do if I was at home. He views a stay at home mother's job as one of the most important purposes one has in life.

Mike is gaining a relationship with Jacob he would have never experienced—*ever.* I know that he will have this special bond with his son as his son will have with him, because of this blessing that came wrapped up in an answered prayer.

Thought 73

Take time to bless and pray for those known and unknown to you. As you pass someone on the street or in your place of work and your eyes can feel their difficulty, send a short blessing. When you see an ambulance speed by or are caught in a traffic jam due to an accident—surround the vehicle and persons in a white light, praying that their journey is a safe one. When you notice a plane in the distant skies, mentally visualize a white band of light around it. It will cost nothing, yet the deed is priceless. It will add a vibrant energy to our planet and those that the light is directed for.

Prayers coming from our heart are like shooting stars rocketing from our crown chakra to the heavens and back. These rays then proceed toward the individuals they were meant for. Remember, no thought goes to waste. Each thought is a unique form of energy that is powerful and creative. The saying 'be careful what you wish for' is very meaningful. Our thoughts and their intentions can have a two-edged sword effect.

When you are in the company of someone difficult or intolerable, visualize a pink or white light entering their crown Chakra or encompassing their body. Pink signifies the aura of divine love. Even if the capacity to send feelings of love, compassion and non-judgment is absent, then concentrate wholly on the aura of pink light encircling them. Ask God to aid in sending warmth and love, as you assist in enshrouding them in a halo of pink or white radiance.

* * *

This story comes from an old soul whose friendship I deeply treasure. Her love and compassion for humanity is a rarity, as is her light to the human race. This is a story about the power of love and the power within each of us. All names have been disguised for privacy purposes.

This is Star's story:

It has never failed that, whenever I approach a situation where I am sending love and white light to whoever I am experiencing difficulty with, it is literally smoothed over the next time I am in their company; or an evident transformation will occur within their nature. I would like to share with you this technique in which I label it 'The Power of Love'.

When I am confronted by situations where I am finding it hard to connect with another person or finding their behavior somewhat intolerable, I take a step back and try to remove myself from the situation. It is at this point that I try to find a moment where I can enter into a more relaxed frame of mind. This is usually done at my home, as this is where I can feel most comfortable and begin to let go.

I enter into a meditative state where I go to my heart. Once I am at the heart chakra, I mentally visualize a connected line to my soul. I take my soul and connect it to that person's soul, which I visualize approximately six inches above their head.

I then unite with that soul by saying, *"please forgive me, as I forgive you and let's form a clear flow."*

At that point I send a beam of white light, which binds to the other soul.

I use white as my form of connecting and transforming the aura of the other individual, however, use whichever feels comfortable for you. Pink is wonderful as it is very soothing. It calms and restores equilibrium in that individual and is the aura of omnipotent love. I use white light because it is like a laser beam—it is almost like sending someone e-mail or hooking up to the internet—it is immediate. When I am sending them white light, I am transmitting a packet of information directed to their soul, upon which they receive instantly.

I am connecting to their soul on the soul's level by saying, *"ok—these two personalities are having problems, let's do what is best for the highest good of all concerned."*

I told this to a cousin of mine who was having a lot of trouble with a woman at work. She told me that she literally wanted to strangle this co-worker. She had tried everything from reasoning to staying out of her way and nothing seemed to work.

I told her, *"well, this may sound a little weird for you, but this is what I use when I am in those situations."*

I explained to her the technique and then I said, *" above all— try to send them love when you are asking for forgiveness and understanding from both souls. Having the love component in it is the key factor."*

She did it and called me back soon after to say that she could not believe it—it actually worked! This co-worker was as nice as she could be and it never went back to the way it was previously. My cousin now uses it frequently on people that she finds difficulty connecting with.

One situation that stands clear in my mind was when I was working in a medical education family practice—residency program. I was working with a man named John Henry who was technically my boss. I had known John for years and, as an observation, he was an immature soul who was extremely insecure with very high ego needs. It was essential for him to be the center of attention at all costs and he needed to take credit even if he was absent or had no part in implementing a project. He and I would butt heads left and right. I often developed something and turned the concept or idea over to him. He would look it over, own it as his, take it to the boss, and receive the praise.

His salary was three times what I was making, and I was the one coming up with his ideas! Needless to say, this built up quite a bit of resentment within me, as he also was at times pompous and abrupt. Well, one day as we were both in a meeting I called his shot and took him down verbally in front of people. Afterwards, I regretted what I had done, as that was not what I was about—I lost my temper, thus, going down to his level.

On reflection, I knew that this was not who I wanted to be, nor was this who or what I was about. I went home and I began to meditate. I proceeded to do the visualization of connecting the heart and soul in the evening and also the next morning before I went to work. I went to my heart and then connected a white band to my soul. Then I visualized John and all that he was. I connected with his soul six inches above his head and, using love as this was the key point, I projected onto him understanding. I asked for forgiveness for my behavior, as I forgave him for who he was, as he was in a certain stage of development in his life. I then asked for the souls to work together. I knew if the souls could work together, it would trickle down into personality and ego. I broke the connection and released it into the Universe. As I set it free, I knew that this was a perfectly peaceful intent.

That morning as I walked into work, I innately felt my heart start to soften. It was no longer hard. He came in and it was amazing. He was as warm and congenial as he could be. There was a kindness and respect that he conveyed to me that was never present before. We had a real connection overnight. After the day I sent him my personal e-mail of white light, he treated me fairly and did not take credit for my ideas or work again. There was no animosity between us any longer. He still did what he did—but he did not do it to me. We both saw each other in a totally different light.

Thought 74

Rituals can be most sacred and enlightening when done with sincere reverence and little expectation. They can also help one become more attuned to one's inner surroundings. Rituals or ceremonies lose their power when presented with some type of expectation, such as bargaining, reward, or spiritual recognition.

I believe that divinity could care less if one lived in an ashram (spiritual hermitage, monastery) for an extended period, was a vegetarian, or meditated three hours a day. What is most important is a daily moment with God and keeping that date with Him each and every day. The time of day or length of time is not what is significant. What is vital is keeping that moment between you and Him constant.

This is one of the highest forms of Self-love, as it keeps the chaos stable. A Puga (ceremony) can only enhance the beauty that is already there. Every day we walk through abundance but sadly, many of us are unaware of its presence.

Reincarnation and Karma, What are They?

" Reincarnation is the process by which the soul evolves; it exists for the growth and development of the soul...reincarnation tells us that we have not come from nothing. Our present condition is the result of what we have made of ourselves from our past."

Sri Chinmoy

Thought 76

Reincarnation is not a new concept. Early Christians, Hasidic Jews and Greek teachers were familiar with this thought and it was widely recognized among them. Each lifetime we set out to correct and learn what we lacked in our previous lives due to ignorance and misdeed. We also set out to achieve unfulfilled desires that we feel to experience for our soul's growth. Karma and reincarnation go hand in hand. What we sow we must reap. The only judgment that comes forth is the one we give to ourselves.

Choices formed create growth and strength for lessons to be learned and relationships to be resolved. *Have you ever wondered why you have the family you have?* Some might say, I would have never chosen such people, they are completely opposite of what I am! Yet, you have chosen them, as they have you. The soul selects circumstances with which to gain knowledge. This allows the soul to relearn an experience or make amends by experiencing what they perpetrated. Not all souls return to relearn or make amends, some choose families in which to teach and have family members form better choices.

Thought 77

Birth is not by chance. We came here because no one else could replace who we are. No one else could replace what we needed to learn and experience. We are each unique and no one could fit the shoe better than you or I. For this reason we chose the country, race, and family in which to gain necessary teachings for the purpose of fulfilling our mission.

Some would say that they would have never chosen such parents. But the parents provide the seeds of opportunity for the soul's development. The choice is in the hands of each soul and some have been shown possible results before incarnating. In the end, we have free will and destiny is decided by each of us, each spirit.

This in no way excuses behaviors such as the abuse of children or diminishes our responsibility to the victim and abuser. It does, however, suggest that they may have chosen this situation due to karma created from a past life. Other possibilities may include rapid soul development or lessons the soul may need to learn in order to make headway in that field and aid others going through similar circumstances. It clarifies some of the mysteries that plague our world and helps us delve into an understanding of why such things occur.

Thought 78

A mentally challenged individual is one where the soul of that being is highly evolved. The choice made by each soul is for rapid spiritual development and perhaps lessons need to be learned. It provides parents and family members growth and enlightenment possibilities within *them-Selves.* Many regard mentally challenged individuals as that, mentally incapable. This is not true. They are more attuned to the inner workings of their being-ness than most of us ever hope to be. Most of their lives they have had to go *with-in*, while most of our lives we were busy being *with-out*.

Thought 79

A soul consists of choice. Every soul *chooses*. That choice may include coming to be in the womb for a short period of time to advance, learn, or teach; or to experience a few days, weeks, or months of life on this plane in order to complete its formation—its evolvement. What may seem as an injustice to one, is part of a continuing journey to another-the Atman (soul).

The will is free, the spirit unbound, no one can own another. We are owned only by the divinity within our own Atman (soul).

* * *

This story comes from a friend, Dr. Roberto Villegas. Dr. Villegas, a Neonatologist recounts a compelling moment in his life caused by a four-week-old patient and mother.

This is Dr. Villegas' story:

Lifetimes are measured not by years, but by how one affects those around them. In my line of work, I have seen how a small life in a short period of time can have a tremendous impact on people. In my years working as a Neonatologist, a little baby boy named David revealed to me his light through his death. David was a premature baby, born weighing about one pound and a few ounces. I met David's mother and had grown attached to both. I remember the events leading up to David's passing. I would give his mother progress reports on his condition. You could imagine with a baby weighing only 500 grams, they are not always going to be fine; many ups and downs will follow. His mother and I shared tears and smiles throughout this ordeal. On one night, David's condition turned for the worse and as God would have it, I was the physician on call. I remember calling his mother to the hospital. She came and sat at the bedside of David. She watched me, as I tried to help David become better. It soon became apparent that this little boy was not going to come around. He was having terrible problems, one of which was that he was bleeding from the lungs. I do not think he was in any pain, but the problems persisted. David struggled on for many hours with each tiny breath. I began to tell his mother very gradually what was going on. Tears started streaming down her face. She soon realized that, what I was telling her, was that her little boy was dying. She started to cry out loud and little by little we could see the heart rate slowing down in his little incubator. I turned to David's mother and asked her if she wanted to carry David. In my heart, I could not see this child dying tied to all the machinery that surrounded his little body. The best thing that I could do was have him die in the arms of his family. I put David in her arms and she started to cry and pray. She prayed in a totally open and uninhibited manner. She was asking God to take care of her little boy—her little David—because he was just a little baby. She knew he was afraid to die, as he struggled to live. She asked God to take care of her son, as he went on his journey. She then gave permission for David's spirit to be released. As she held David in her arms, she told him how strong he was for having lived so long. She told him not to be afraid. She told him that he struggled and fought hard and what a good little warrior he was. She whispered to him that God was going to take care of him now—and not to worry, but to go. David passed on fifteen minutes later.There are times when as a physician I feel that I am a good vehicle for taking care of babies. Other times it becomes too much, as I will have two, three or sometimes four children dying. It is in those hours when I tell God that I cannot do it anymore and it is in those instances that I do not see death for awhile. Nevertheless it picks up again, but in those moments I am able to gather strength and courage. I am convinced that this time is made available for me to search, digest and understand certain events at whatever limited level I can comprehend them.

I have come to believe and accept that God does not give our soul more than we can handle.

Thought 78

Karma is our creation produced from our actions and the consequences of those actions. Every day a choice is made, leading that person down a different pathway. It is through our choices that karma arises. We are intertwined with the decisions made by us. Before we act, we must ask ourselves, what will this action create?

If, in our hearts we see goodness— then we should continue. If we feel otherwise, we must ask ourselves why are we doing it? This is the meaning of karma. Karma is not a bad or good thing—karma is an expansion of who we are—it is a soul thing. And it will never let us get away with anything. We are all here to contribute to our planet—not deduct from it.

Thought 80

Let's not use the excuse *"it's my karma"* for not taking responsibility. Karma has become a loosely used expression pitched around like a ball. If you have an addiction such as drinking, smoking, food, or drugs, is it your karma to drink, smoke, overeat, or get high throughout your lifetime?

By creating such imbalances in our emotional and physical Self, we give birth to another lifetime of trying to overcome what we failed to do in this incarnation. Instead of thinking that this is my karma, one should look at how best this pattern be broken.

Maybe it is your karma to master this addiction by abstinence.

Thoughts, and their Potency

"The thought manifests as the word.
The word manifests as the deed.
The deed develops into a habit,
And the habit hardens into character.
So watch the thought and its ways with care,
And let it spring from love, Out of respect for all beings."
Buddhist aphorism

Thought 81

Life can be a banquet yet so many starve! The choice is in our hands—we can either abstain or reach into the abundant Universe for our share! All it takes is the removal of habitual thinking!

What we truly feel deep within our center attracts what we truly want. When we find the 'I Am' of who we are, acknowledge its existence, only then can we recognize certain thought patterns that we adhere too. This is the first step to satisfying a needless hunger.

Thought 82

We are beings of energy and this vibration fills our frame. Our Consciousness is connected to every cell throughout our body. This energy vibration can be seen through a process known as Kirlian photography, which distinguishes energy patterns on photos in different areas of our body; one being the hand.

The difference in energy can be seen between a hand that is thinking or sending positive thoughts, compared to a hand that may not be. This energy field that surrounds our physical body is called our aura.

Our aura can indicate a weakness even before it has been reflected in our physical body. Our Consciousness creates a change in our energy field and this change is manifested in our aura before symptoms occur in the physical body. Consequently, it is the aura that affects and changes the physical body. The end result being that our physical body begins with direction from our Consciousness. This leads us to recognize *thought before form.*

Thought 83

Have you ever wondered why certain people bring out a more positive mood in you, although sometimes you may not feel so wonderful? Or why in their presence are your spirits always uplifted? On the other hand have you pondered why other individuals can sometimes make you feel drained and fatigued in spite of doing nothing to instigate it? This is due to the aura that surrounds each one of us. The energy patterns from each person are being fed from the thought patterns that are formed by them.

Consequently, when you are in the presence of someone whose energy pattern may not blend with yours, you will feel it. As your aura blends with theirs, some of their energy vibrations will be brought into your energy vibrations. As a mutual exchange of energies overlap and intermingle, it will disclose to our super conscious mind the energy tones of that individual. Hence, at times, before you get a chance to know an individual, your sense has already done the job!

Thought 84

Every day, more doubts than affirmations run through our mind. Think about it. How many times will your actions be second-guessed before thinking positively about them? I can't do this, I am not ready to do that, I am not good enough for this person, it takes so much longer to grasp a concept, and so on and so on.

When we think affirmatively about who we are, we unblock gates that we ourselves have created. We tap into our highest good, which sets the flow for the metaphysical law of radiation and attraction to begin. An affirmation said with true knowing that God has already provided for and not said to produce a wanting, will manifest great results.

Take heed to our thoughts—as they create who we are. We make the world we live in by the thoughts and words that are formed from these energies. There are many examples of affirmations. Use one that feels most comfortable and right for you. It can be something you have formed through feelings and experiences. When the connection between the heart and throat chakra is impenetrable, it is then that the umbilical cord to our five senses is cut and manifestation emanates.

* * *

I have come to understand that we are the makers of our lives. We create a continuum of realities by how we process our thoughts. Self-pity can be a strong downward vibration, always pulling your energies *out* and not enabling you to focus *in*. I found that if we permit self-pity and like behaviors to infiltrate our Atman (oneness, soul) we will live that life attracting like circumstances and like opportunities.

For sometime, I was consumed by self-pity and was envious of others for a variety of reasons. I asked myself why has God given me the raw end of the deal? *Why me?* I had little choice one day but to face the issues that were driving me to the point of anguish, envy, and unsatisfaction.

I slowly understood that by allowing yourself to grow weeds, you are giving them permission to blossom. But by taking the time, energy, and persistence to pluck them at their very roots, you can prevent future ones from growing, manifesting a weed free garden.

Like the garden full of weeds, I had to ask myself—*who am I*? Do I want to remain a field full of dandelions or do I choose to manifest into a rose garden? For numerous people, this can be difficult to get past. To look beyond the *Me* and the *I*, acquires time, energy, and persistence. Most of all, it requires a Self-love that we all are capable of having, though for many, can be buried beneath the soil.

How does one maintain a weed free garden? It starts with a willingness to listen, unlearn, and understand your Atman (soul), without becoming defensive, blaming or rationalizing your behavior. Gaining knowledge in the spiritual arena by reading and spending time with the Self, permits you to become familiar with your internal world. We live in two realities—the outer and inner dimensions, each with its own set of principles.

These two worlds must blend. In order to do so, one needs imagination and inspiration. Without imagination, we are our own prisoners, chained to a mind that cannot see beyond the physical. This is where ignorance is cultivated. With imagination, our sixth Chakra (third eye) will awaken, taking us into the eyes behind our mind. This is the realm of the Beyond, where a breath stands between our dimension and theirs.

Without inspiration, our development will be restrained. We will live with little contentment, unable to be satisfied and continually wanting. With inspiration, this hole is filled. One need not search anymore because what was discovered was always present. There is no achievement, only awakening. The only search one will persevere is the continued quest for completion of the Self.

By making our world *with-in* more important than the world *with-out*, we are on the path to Nirvana (enlightenment).

Thought 85

Anger. We all have experienced this type of emotion in some manner or another, either as a sudden flare up or one that is slow and steady, building over a long period of time. Quick anger is preferable to one that simmers, as it dissipates rather rapidly.

Nevertheless, any act of anger is like a ripple in a pond. The original "angry person's" vibrations will trickle down to several people, similar to a domino effect. Those who come into contact with these vibrations will in turn be affected, thus adding more negative vibrations to the planet as a whole. Do we really need to do this to our earth and ourselves?

Negative thinking just brings us closer to influencing ill health and like circumstances. If we understood how negative thought patterns worked, we would connect the dots back to the source—which is our substance of thought.

Humankind has a responsibility to unlearn—and to think differently. The disasters that plague our earth could be lessened with a collective consciousness that permeated more goodness, acceptance, and realization of Self.

Thought 86

We are unlimited like the air we inhale and the ocean from which we drink. There is no limit to our bounty. We are creators: we choose with our thoughts what we want to build upon, grow, and master. Frivolous, scattered, and fearful thoughts will bring forth frivolous, scattered, and fearful results. We are a magnet, mentally projecting goodness, success, or failure unto others or ourselves. Remember, for success to be successful, it had to be mentally pictured first!

Thought 87

Thoughts, attitudes and emotions are substances. They are self creative energy bundles that reflect what our aura is made of. The thought is then turned into a sound vibration. If the energy and sound are done with a *knowing-ness* or strong faith that the task is attainable, transformation will materialize.

The conviction that it will be actualized will give birth to an intense power of the *thought* and the *word*. Thanking in advance is the most significant ritual, and is key for completion and manifestation. To be grateful before the deed is done is an essential part to materialization.

The Master of our Tongue...

Before you speak, ask yourself,
is it kind, is it necessary,
is it true, does it improve on the silence?
Sri Sathya Sai Baba

Thought 88

Words must be carefully constructed before they are voiced. Unlike written words, the tongue is similar to an arrow. Once it is shot, it cannot be retrieved. Placing a filter between our thoughts and words allows a moment for enlightenment where if necessary, filtration may transpire.

Thought 89

The best-kept secret is the one you share with yourself. What might seem as an exchange of innocent information or may deem complimentary to another—may not be so for the listener.

Gossiping can leave us with an essence of emptiness and discontentment. Although the moment may induce feelings of authority, as you have caught the attention of others, soon your innerness will emanate feelings of guilt. This is a sign that our soul transmits to us, when actions are contrary to the Atman (divinity).

When we look at our intercommunication as a human race, we have a lot to learn about the power of the tongue. For many, it would take one negative aspect for the focus of the dialogue to alter its course. How interesting would the conversation be if all one did was talk about the positive aspects of another?

Human nature is such that we find it far more engaging to hear faultfinding evaluations of another, then solely concentrate on their goodness. At the end one must keep in mind that harmless gossip rarely remains benign.

Thought 90

Gentleness and a sweet tongue can provide most of what one needs to thrive on. There is no greater form of communication than a voice whose tone is soothing—and its ears always listening.

Thought 91

Listen! Listen! Listen! Very few of us actually listen. A skill highly in demand, but few qualified for the job. There is enormous joy in listening. It gives you, the listener, the power of Self-control and a sense of thoughtfulness. The receiver will immediately feel the residue of your ease. You will find that by listening, a magnetic quality will arise within you. Your need to wait for your turn to speak will cease. You will actually take delight in lending your ear!

Thought 92

Rapid speech brings about strewn thoughts. Take time when you speak. There is no need to hurry along your communication. It only distresses the receiver and deposits more confusion in your message. Like an IV drained of its substance to aid the sick, so is the tongue, when thoughts fleet at a pace that leaves the listener depleted and fatigued.

* * *

This story comes from an experience I had with a lady whom I will call Susan.

This is my story:

Susan came to my home to discuss doing some volunteer work on a project that I was working on. After pleasantries were exchanged, we settled down to converse on what needed to get done for this particular project. Before I had a chance to say anything, her pace of speech accelerated, becoming extremely difficult to understand. Each sentence took much concerted listening effort. I tried to understand most of what she said, but when A point need to be made, she would interrupt with her opinion or idea on the subject. I thought she was a very nice woman by nature, but I began to feel extremely drained and fatigued by her pitch and rate of speech. I remember sitting and watching her mouth open and close at such a rapid pace. I kept thinking to myself, how does she do it. Every so often I would rear her back onto the intended subject, as she would go off on tangents talking on unrelated issues. There came a point in the conversation, where only a third of her words were being heard, as I filtered the rest. By the end of the meeting. I was completely depleted. The point to this story was that by the end of the meeting, I really did not know if I could or wanted to work with Susan. The volunteer work was important for her career; to give her a start in the field she eventually wanted to pursue. I knew that if I did decide to work with her, I would need to gently speak to her about her communication. I did find out later from the individual who referred her to me, that in unfamiliar situations she would become anxious, which resulted in babbling. I soon realized how true that was, as she seemed so much more settled when I met with her the next time.

Nevertheless, some people never get that second chance. Whether it is a job interview, prospective date, business meeting or social gathering, one needs to be aware of how they speak.

When one starts on the path to meditation, the patterns of speech will evolve within themselves. As we blend the exoteric within the esoteric, we begin to sense the empathy and gentleness in our choice of language and our tones. We recognize that at times, silence can be the best form of compassion, viewing silent patches in conversations no longer as a discomfort. So too, our awareness of others heightens, and we are able to discern the right time to bring forth a conversation that will seem amendable for listening.

Conversely, our inner reality will convey to us the appropriateness of our communication. If attuned to our inner workings, a warm sense will take form in our heart. Leaving us to remember the timely and befitting nature of our spoken words.

Universality of Religions, Different Truths

"Religion, like poetry, is not a mere idea; it is an expression. The self expression of God is an endless variedness of creation; and our attitude towards the Infinite Being must also in its expression have a variedness of individuality, ceaseless and unending."

Tagore

Lesson 93

The greatest place of worship where one can enter at anytime and where race, creed, or religion play no significant role are the temple of our minds. This is our God-Mind. When we understand that divinity lives within each of us and that one of the highest forms of love is the love of our Atman (soul); only then will we begin to accept our differences as we do our similarities.

Only then can we achieve freedom by shattering the chains of intolerance. And only then can the spirit of truth be embraced for its common aspects as well as its variances.

Remember, there is not *one* door to God, but several. For as many races, creeds, and cultures tend this earth, there are many different roads leading to Him. Each is unique, but all searching for the same Being.

It is in our hearts and with our consciousness that our halo soars, no matter what external method is applied.

* * *

This story comes from a gentleman whom I had the opportunity to meet while sitting next to him on a flight. I was asked to give up my seat in order that a family could sit together and I obliged. In doing so, I had a wonderful conversation with this gentleman named Rajiv.

This is Rajiv's story:

He relayed to me his story about acceptance and toleration. I am of East Indian origin and my wife, American. We met purely by chance, if there is such a thing. I had a very good friend in college who was in the MBA program with me, he was going down to see his fiancée, who happened to be going to school in a town about thirty miles away. He asked me if I wanted to come with him and I declined, saying that I needed to work. He did not take no for an answer and said he would buy me dinner. I accepted right away! Being a student, free food will make me go anywhere! I went down with him and my wife was his fiancée's roommate. We all went out to dinner and hit it off. A few months later, I went to Idaho to meet with her parents. Frankly, I was a little apprehensive, as I did not know how they would react to me. I was welcomed and accepted immediately without any reservations. Two years later, I asked her father's permission to marry his daughter. He gave his consent and we set a date. We went to my fiancée's place of worship where we met with the man who was going to marry us. He said he was willing to marry the two of us, if I accepted his form of God, wholly and completely. This was not something that I did not expect, after all he was doing his job, but at the same time I could not lie to him. I responded by saying, *"I believe faith is very important in a person's life. I think faith, and the acceptance of God is vital, no matter what name you call that God. The reason for my belief is because I come from a culture in India where we have so many Gods, every little sect has their own belief system. We teach that one should lead a good life, respecting one's fellow human beings, irrespective of belief system.*

The differing religions all prescribe this way of life, and most are accepting of the other Gods. If one believes in the God Vishnu, and the other believes in the God Rama, it does not mean one or the other is a bad person. I have seen a lot of conflict come from people who believe that their God is the only God and that it does not matter how you live your life". I went on to say, *"perhaps I come from a culture where riots have killed many people in the past, all in the name of God and I do not think this is right. I think God looks to see if you are a good person and how you lead your life towards family and fellow human kind".* I looked at him expecting him to nod approvingly and smile; after all, this is what causes many religious conflicts and wars. Instead his face became sterner and sterner. I continued on by saying *"I do believe God is a vital part of our existence, but it should not matter what name you call God."* I looked hoping for a smile, but his expression was solemn. At that point I knew something was wrong, as I really thought he would be approving of this philosophy. I then let him speak and he told me that in his faith there is only one way to reach heaven, and that was through worshipping their form of what they considered to be God. At this time I was quite confused, as this did not make much sense to me. So I responded by saying, *" there are billions of people around the world who worship different forms of God. They are very good, honest, loving human beings, the kind that you and I would want to know and meet. Are you telling me that they are all going to hell?"*

He looked me straight in the eye and without a hesitation said, *"yes."*

At this point I was at a complete loss for words. I was definitely upset, but I did not want to show it. I did not want to ruin my fiancée's relationship with members of her place of worship. I said, *"Okay, I will think about that"*. I needed, however, to voice one more thing before I left, so I turned around and said, *"it just does not make sense to me that a God or someone you call a God does not care whether you are a good person or a bad person. Furthermore, it does not make sense that you would be banished to hell if you did not accept Him in the correct form. If this is the case, this does not seem to be a reasonable God. Maybe I am too rationale, but I don't think that there is such a punishing God"*. Well, he did not like that and said that he has to believe that I have accepted his faith before he could marry us. We left the meeting and I turned to my fiancée and said, *"listen, I am sorry, I know you want to get married at this church but I cannot lie to him. Next time we meet with this man, and if he turns to me and asks if I have accepted his faith as the only faith to get to heaven, I am going to have to say no. I cannot look him in the eye and lie, I just cannot do that"*. My fiancée turned to me and said, *"that is fine Rajiv, I accept that. If we have to find another church we will, or we will give up the church wedding altogether"*. It was quite unfortunate, but three weeks before the wedding, my fiancée's father was killed in a car accident. We were so busy with the funeral that we never got a chance to go back. I called and told the preacher that things were crazy right now and asked him if we were still on for the wedding?

He said, *"yes, yes, you just go and take care of the family things."*

The day of the wedding I turned to my fiancée and told her that if he asks me before the wedding ceremony if I have accepted his form of God, I am not going to lie to him. I am going to say that I believe God can be called by many names in many forms. He never did address that question to me. He went ahead and performed the ceremony. We had a wonderful wedding, in the lovely little white church that my wife always wanted to get married in, and that question never came up again.

The lesson I have taken with me is that there are intolerant views coming from the most unlikely places. When I turned to this man the first time and told him that people should lead good lives, I truly expected him to be pleased with this. For me, this is what I expect a person in charge of a place of worship to preach. We should lead a good life, not be judgmental of others, and help our fellow humans. Instead, his message seemed to be to believe in his faith as the only way to go to heaven and make sure that one attended his place of worship every Sunday. If one did not do this, then one would go to hell.

Although my son is only four years old, I hope to instill in him the attitude of acceptance. I do not want him to tolerate, as that is just putting up with another individual's belief system. I want him to understand and put into practice, as he goes through his life that it is how one conducts and lives life. It is not what one does for an hour a week or a couple of hours a day; it is what one does every minute of their life that is significant.

Thought 94

When fear is instilled as respect in an organization or religion, the result can lead to an internal breakdown within that structure. When one faith claims sole proprietorship to God or when intolerance of other religions and cultures predominate to the exclusion of others, this may guide many followers to disillusionment. True spirituality is birthed from freedom and not from co-dependency driven by power and control. This is where the manifestation of cults are born, as those discontented within their system look for other alternatives to find solace in.

If followers from the religions of the world practiced what their great teachers taught and lived, we would live in a different frame of consciousness today. Many would find this wakefulness hard to accept, as we would live in a world where little religious conflict would reign. We must come to the realization that we ALL come from separate realities. And that the only judgment that holds any weight by our separateness, is how to be the best in kindness, acceptance, and the love we have for Self and humankind. We must keep in mind that each religion makes up one part of the whole. Each part being a vital addition, not a subtraction to the One Universal truth—which is God.

The more spiritually evolved will go beyond one truth and witness different truths in the religions of the world. While the less spiritually evolved will remain within the shores of difference and separateness.

Thought 95

We all have heard or been taught that we should not judge another, nor caste the first stone. But how many of us resist that urge: *very few*. To judge or criticize others is a waste of ones vitality. Learn that minding your own business leaves time to concentrate on the Self and the growth of your inner wisdom and spirituality. *Sometimes being opinion-less is not a bad place to be in!*

I believe that what you judge, you someday become. The stone you cast will someday be thrown at you, while the words you use, will someday be used back at you. So instead of jumping to conclusions with angry thoughts, try to remain *reaction-free*. Creating anger and judgmental energies only gives way for negative thought forms to surround and infiltrate your body cells—for what? Something you may learn later was a misunderstanding or for circumstances not fully known. The energies we send out are like a circle, 180 degrees, they are re-routed and head back in our direction.

Thought 96

There are many individuals who consider themselves loving, religious people. Yet those same people, when faced with persons of differing beliefs or who do not live within the guidelines of what they believe to be a conforming lifestyle, are not so loving or accepting.

They read words from holy books, which they interpret as God's, yet, with those same words only judgment, contempt, and intolerance are voiced. What they selectively forget by judging and condemning another is that they judge and condemn the very God they declare to love! For God resides in the very breath of each man, woman, and child, regardless of lifestyle and beliefs.

Blasphemy evolves when we tolerate and do not accept. For in toleration we are putting up with another person's belief system, although we think that it is wrong. Hence, we *allow* them to live by tolerating their lifestyle, beliefs and religion. *Who are we to tolerate?*

Each human has a Divine right. This Divine right grants each individual to live in acceptance, respect, and individuality. You may not agree, but you are not living their life. You may deem your view as truth, but that is your truth. You must allow yourself to behold another's difference, not as a difference, but as another approach to living life.

Thought 97

When we look at strife, violence, and fear, many would blame religious conflict. But if one took time to reflect, they would realize that this anger and war-like behavior is not caused by religion, but by the selfishness and greed of man.

In many countries where one religion presides, there is still war raging between the two. The sad aspect is that they use the name of religion to incite harm against humankind. The essence of all religions is based upon *Oneness.* Learnedness of a religious doctrine does not make one a Master. Mastering the scriptures, whether it is in the form of the Bible, Bhagavad Gita, Koran, Dhammapada, or Torah etc., is possible for the one who looks upon all religions with equanimity and respect. When this principle of love can be fertilized and *exclusivity* eliminated—only then will strife, violence and fear cease to bloom.

If we cannot get past small barriers such as respect and acceptance of diverse religions within our own small communities, how can we even begin to see the big picture? How can we hope for serenity within the nations of the world, when we have a hard time accepting our neighbor's diversity?

Food, a Way of Life

"Know when you eat that all food is God's body. Your eating should be a sacrifice. When you eat, you should think, "I am eating to gather energy, to better serve others". Whatever you eat, offer it to God and see the Lord in it."

Swami Satchidananda

Thought 98

Offer to share a piece of your food with who ever dines with you; especially if they have not brought their own. While you enjoy the company of each other, share a small piece of what you have. When you offer a part of your meal to another, you offer a part of yourself that is God given. Food is a part of God, and humankind grew in the womb from that very substance. We are all Gods and Goddesses relearning our divinity and part of that divinity is birthed from the substance from which we were formed.

In India, one never leaves a home without some type of offering from the host. If one declines food or drink, the custom is to offer a little sugar for them to eat. A guest leaves with a small part of the host's graciousness and always with a sweet taste in one's mouth.

* * *

Although brought up in the West, we were always taught that if a guest enters your home or if you are outside the home, you must never eat without offering to your fellow man first. You would first ask another before you indulge yourself. The same principle applies at home. Do not ask your guests what you can get them, as many will say they are fine. Instead, bring them your offering as part of your hospitality. Numerous times when you enter an East Indian home, they will ask the question, *"Do you prefer tea, coffee or a cold drink?"* The question is not left open ended as *"what can I get you?"* Upon answering, you will usually see some type of food set on the table for the person to enjoy. Innumerable times, when friends or acquaintances visited, many expressed surprise and gratitude at the hospitality. I remember thinking how unfortunate it is to be surprised at another's graciousness and how unfortunate it is that we find ourselves expecting so little from each other. One might ask the question, why is this important to me? This is a different culture and in the West we do things differently. Being bicultural, I found that it did make a difference in the treatment of another and in how I felt about *who* I was. When you offer a part that is yours to another, you give a part of your heart. You give a piece of yourself. That piece is your Atman (inner divinity). This inner divinity is your soul which strengthens our interconnectedness to one another.

Thought 99

Our body is our temple. When we fast, we allow for elimination of toxins from our system. Fasting twice a month will aid in cleaning and revitalizing your temple. Once you are comfortable with fasting, try once a week, taking only water or fruit juices— no dairy products. Breaking the fast is just as important. Do not eat a large meal. One must break the fast with something light. Your body is similar to a car. You would not run your car at a careless speed soon after it came from the repair shop. Rather, you would ease the engine into a moderate rate before hitting the speed you wish to attain.

Eating must be worked in slowly. The aim of fasting is for the good health of your body. That is why most religions practice some type of fast during their holy days. Regardless of religion or spiritual practice, fast for the health of your well-being.

Thankfulness

"With the awakening of the dawn and the lotus buds, my soul softly opens in prayer to receive Thy light."
Paramahansa Yogananda

Thought 100

Each morning as you awaken to a new day, thank God for this beginning. Request Him to bless this day and all activities that evolve from it. You will expose your essence to a more serene and confident rhythm, where each note will flow more steadily into the next. And as the utilization of your energy system consolidates with your core sense of power—you will feel enlivened. This act of gratitude merges our non-physical Self to our point of power—in the timeless dimension of *now*.

As you end the day and lay to sleep, repeat the same. The results will return you to your Self by remembering who you were and where came from.

Thought 101

Give thanks each day for the gift of life. Many of us walk this planet half-heartedly, never fully appreciating or understanding the significance of what a new day brings or the loved ones that surround our lives.

The implementation of gratitude is necessary in every experience, however pleasant or unpleasant it may have been. Our soul does not take on more then what we can handle, and nothing ever happens to us without the soul's permission.

We need to grasp that every problem and every success falls within our control. Losses, sorrow, pain, and worries are examinations in the school of life. They reveal to us our weaknesses and develop the fortitude, patience, and endurance to cognize stability within the chaos.

We must love our life today, accepting the package of who we are in the present, not the package of who we hope to be in a distant tomorrow.

* * *

This story comes from a certified exercise specialist named Nancy Norris whom I have had the pleasure of knowing. Her story makes us aware of the bigger picture in life—and brings light unto issues that one might think are enormous but in actuality is quite small. This is the paradox in which life is lived, and this is Nancy's story.I feel that we are here on Earth for a purpose. We have this purpose even before we incarnate. I believe that God has a plan for us right from the very beginning. I give credence to predestination, but I also believe that there can be changes made in our life. It depends on what we do with the choices laid before us.

There is a big plan and a big picture. I feel what we do and how we handle life's situations can alter that picture just a bit. It is similar to how an architect designs a house. There might be changes made to the house throughout its lifetime, but the basic draft is somewhat the same. This is how I envision my life.

I came to this realization after working with so many different kinds of people in the fitness business; beginning with fitness classes and personal training, to working as a brain injury specialist with clients who have had severe brain trauma from accidents.

I think what troubles me most is the fact that people try to be something they are not. I speak to various individuals each day and it seems that they have a vision in their heads of what they want to look like, *not so much what they are.* People forget to look at who they are on the inside—focusing heavily on the outward. I am not stating that one does not need the externals to help meet one's goals, but it seems that many are forgetting their goodness, warmth, and contribution to society. They overlook the growth of their children and nurturing of their families. Many become too caught up in the outside, which leaves them rarely satisfied and content inside. I was working with a woman who was six feet tall, blonde and beautiful. She was a larger woman who weighed about two-hundred-and-forty pounds. We were working on weight loss, as she was totally frustrated by not being able to lose the weight. Because she weighed two-hundred-and-forty pounds one might think that she was an unhealthy person, but she was not. Her cholesterol was low and she exercised appropriately. So I began thinking about this lady who had come to me for help and how she seemed frustrated with her whole life—not just the weight. We sat down and talked. She told me that she had a wonderful husband, a terrific career, and all her children were prospering in their lives. She had beautiful and healthy grandchildren, a lovely home, and she contributed enormously to society where she volunteered for a number of wonderful charity organizations. After much thought, I finally said to her that I thought we were focusing so much on the two-hundred-and-forty pounds, that we totally lost sight of some very important facets in her life. She was beautiful, intelligent, happily married, had healthy children and grandchildren, a fulfilling and exciting job, and a lovely home. All of what the Universe blessed her with seemed nonexistent, as the two of us concentrated on that particular figure-two-hundred-and-forty. Consequently, we looked at her diet and changed a few things so she would be eating healthier. I set her on a good exercise routine and began concentrating on being healthy—not thin. In order to achieve the weight loss she desired—we took everything into consideration, the mental, emotional, spiritual, and physical Selves of who she was.

These days when I speak to organizations on health and fitness, I never fail to mention that healthy and fit bodies come in all shapes and sizes. I reached this perspective many years ago by looking at my own body and trying to be as healthy as I could. I soon realized that as healthy as I ate and as much exercise as I got, I was given this body and genetically this was my body. Now can we improve our fitness and health? Yes, we can, but to make drastic changes on the shape of our body will probably not happen. For many years, I worked on trying to make those changes. When I started counseling other people on weight management and having them focus more inwardly, I began to question my own beliefs. Sometimes it is easier to give people advice than it is to take it yourself. The more I heard myself talking to other people about looking within and the more they started to listen, understand and agree with the concept, the more I had to take a good look at what I was doing with my own advice. My youngest daughter had an eating disorder when she was sixteen. This fortunately only lasted for six months. However, to this day despite her being very healthy, she still frets about her weight although she is only five foot four and weighs one-hundred-and-three pounds. About six months ago, she called me and told me that she had put on five pounds.

I said, *" Oh—so now you weigh one hundred and eight"*, and we started laughing. I told her to look at the bigger picture in life, I asked her, *"are you happy?"*

She said, *"yes, I am very happy"*.

I continued by saying, *"you just got a brand new job that is very satisfying and you are in a very healthy happy relationship—life has been good...your life is wonderful and yet you are spending the majority of your time today worrying about five pounds. You know—we really need to look at the greater picture in life rather than focusing on that"*. Every once in a while God will throw this in my face and it really keeps me in touch with who I am and my purpose in this life.Early in the morning is when I do most of my introspection and contemplate about the clients whom I am going to see that day. Everyday, I tell myself that I want to make a difference and that I want to say something that will make them feel good about who they are. Occasionally, we get so caught up in life that we simply forget what and who we really are. I work with some marvelous individuals, especially my head injury clients. They deal on a daily basis with a multitude of issues. One issue is realizing that what they pictured life to be before the accident may be altered now, and possibly a different path must be sought out. The majority of them have a very tough time with this, as they look back at what their life used to be and realize that it will never be that way again. This hits me in such a way that I have little choice but to face my own life and say to myself on a daily basis that *I have no problems—I -absolutely -have- no -problems.* Just this morning I was working with a man who had been married only two years when he had his accident. He and his wife had such dreams about their life and what their future would be together. They were coming home from a ski trip when another car crossed the centerline and hit them head on. She did not sustain any head injuries, however, she had traumatic injuries; but to make a long story short, she healed and has now returned to a very normal life. Nevertheless, she is now helping to take care of a husband who will never walk without a walker or will never be able to go out into the community and work as he had done previously. Every day we work not only on physical activities to keep him strong, but also work on his cognitive skills. From time to time, he will say to me that some days it is really hard as he wishes to be the man he was before the accident. I say to him, *"let's look at the man you are now—and let's see what you can do in a day. Look at how many lives you touch everyday with the man you are at this moment."* I tell him how he inspires so many individuals in the fitness club. Many who have not even been through what he has gone through find him an inspiration. They walk in here feeling that they cannot exercise and then they see him in here every day. I tell him that this is just one small part of his spirit that he gives to others since the accident.

What I have learned and continue to discover from these experiences is that my problems do not seem so large after all. There is a plan and no matter what comes to me this afternoon or tomorrow, I am a stronger person for it. I especially find this inner strength through working with my head injury clients. The patience that seemed hard to bring forth has now become a part of my life. I have to be stronger for them and I believe that makes my power within shimmer more in every aspect of my own life. I feel that one can conquer anything if a healthy spirit is developed. This means that we must be content with the Spirit who dwells inside before we can touch anyone else's Spirit. In helping them to see what good they have, it helps me to look at myself. I am able to see areas that I am good in and areas that I can improve upon. It aids me in striving to be a better person. By helping others to take a deeper look inside them, I have begun to take a deeper look into myself. I have a very good life, and I try to live each day to the fullest, whether it is the fullest for myself or in helping somebody else. We do not know how long we have; every moment should be relished.

One thing that I started doing is rock and mountain climbing. Up high in the mountains it is so peaceful and there are not many people up there, so you have time to reflect on life. It's ironic how small we seem when we look up at the snowy mountain peaks, the sky, stars, and the moon. Being in this atmosphere has made me digest more about who created all of this. I get this overwhelming feeling of how minute things really are in the whole scheme of things. I believe that when one goes through some type of pain in life one becomes more susceptible to empathy. Like many, loss has been a part of my life and it does have an affect on me whether I want it or not. I have been guilty of this and maybe we all are, but I have taken so much for granted. When I look at my clients, especially the ones with the brain injuries, I say to myself, I cannot take this nice life for granted, because it could change within a millisecond. I am finding as I mature, I think less and less of what will make Nancy Norris happy and realize that when I do something that helps improve another human life, I am in some way rewarded immensely. I do not think so heavily about what is going to make me happy anymore. I now find happiness without focusing on it.

Altering Our Consciousness, a Step at a Time

"What can be gained by thinking about the scriptures? What fools! They think themselves to death with information about the path, but never take the plunge!"

Ramakrishna

Thought 102

So many of us sit back and watch things from afar, unwilling to become a *player* due to fear, judgment, and reprisal. But imagine this scenario, if one out of every ten people took a step forward and embraced the role of *player*, I believe we would live in a different state of mindfulness today.

Changing the world in small steps, without the fear of needing to create big steps, is all that is required. Part of being a *player* is not having the need to make it public. You can change a piece of our Earth's consciousness by simply not being the audience.

* * *

A friend named Mercedes runs a business in the food industry.

This is Mercedes' story:

On our way home my husband and I decided to stop off at a local restaurant for dinner. After ordering our meal, we sat for approximately twenty-five minutes, when a gentleman carrying a takeout order came from outside towards the bar. He proceeded to give the food back to the barmaid, who realized she had given him the wrong order.Thirty-five minutes later, a woman walked in to pick up her takeout order. The barmaid picked up the bag that the gentleman had returned and proceeded to show it to the woman. I could tell it was some type of salad meal and the lady nodded in approval of the order. As I sat there, I turned to my husband and said, *"she is going to give her the food that the guy just brought back in"*. My husband replied, *"well, it is none of our business."* I responded by saying, "*she cannot do that, because it is against the law and the health department."* My husband responded by saying, *"you are not going to go over there and tell her that."* I got up from my chair, walked over to the barmaid and said, "*it is against the law what you are doing, you cannot give her this food that the gentleman just returned. You must be aware that once any type of food leaves an establishment, it is a violation of the health code when given to another person*". The customer thanked me for informing her and I returned to my seat. My husband gave me one of his disapproving looks. Nevertheless, I stood my ground because I believed in what I was doing. I watched as the barmaid handed the lady her money back. I feel that it is important that we should try to make an effort to help whenever we can, however inconsequential the act may appear. For it may not be so for the individual involved. I was not trying to be brave or create a scene; it was a matter of ideals that I believed in and try each day to emulate in my own life.

Law of Abundance

"Those who realize the Self are always satisfied. Having found the source of joy and fulfillment they no longer seek happiness from the external world. They have nothing to gain or lose by any action; neither people nor things can affect their security."

Bhagavad Gita

Thought 103

Focusing on what we do not have rather than our abundance, will generally leave us where we began—wanting.

* * *

This story comes from Mary, a lady I had met while I browsed the shelves of the local bookstore where she worked. This is a story that goes beyond the pain and loss of a loved one. This story is about having had the opportunity to love and be loved unconditionally.

This is Mary's story:

When my husband John and I first got married we bought a male cocker spaniel named "John Boy's Shadow". We named him after my husband as he used to follow John everywhere. About a year later, my husband decided that John-boy needed a playmate, so he went and got Cricket, a female cocker spaniel. Cricket and John-boy soon had a litter.

There were five puppies in the litter and of the five puppies we kept one whom we named "Ginger Snap of Shamrock". The reason we kept her is because she chose us. Whenever anybody came to the house to look at the puppies she would hide. She would go underneath the table and peek meekly out with those big mellow eyes. We ended up calling her snapper because of her saucy little personality. She was just the most endearing little puppy one could be blessed to have. She was joy personified.

The third week in July 1999 seemed surreal. It was a time in my life when I was in the process of coming to the end of a job that turned out to be very stressful, leaving me emotionally weak. It was also around the same time that JFK's plane was missing, there just seemed to be a lot of negative energy in the air. We had Snapper for six glorious years and in all that time she was in the pink of health. She had just completed a checkup with nothing irregular to report.

Thursday of that week, Snapper stopped eating and my husband John had mentioned it to me on Friday. I took Snapper to the vet the following day, which was Saturday. The veterinarian diagnosed her with autoimmune hemolytic anemia. This meant that her autoimmune system was messed up and her liver and spleen were becoming infected. The vet said it was treatable and Snapper was put on medication immediately. I was to bring her back in a week. I had to make sure she was eating and drinking. Although this had the potential of being fatal, it was something that he had good luck in treating.

Through the course of that week I had tried to feed her, but her appetite was virtually non-existent. Nevertheless, Snapper would take some food from my hand, as if she knew that would make me happy. It was heartbreaking to see her make that effort. I took her back to the vet that following Friday and her results had shown that she was improving. Her red blood cells had increased and this was a good sign. We just needed to continue the medication.

Oddly enough, when we got back from the vet that day, Snapper's actions were that of a dog trying to absorb all the surroundings she knew and loved dearly. She went inside our house and walked to every place she had been and laid down in as if for the last time. My husband said that she was trying to get comfortable, but when I looked at her she seemed as though she was looking to remember.

I left for work right after the vet's visit and my husband told me that she had stopped eating and drinking, despite his efforts. Around 7:30 p.m. Snapper came up to John and nuzzled his hand. She then licked John's hand, walked across the living room to her mothers crate and went in. A few minutes later John heard a thud, he looked over and she was gone. John ran over to the crate, checked for a pulse and found none. He got her out of the cage, cradled her in his arms as she soaked up all his tears. John later told me that he was convinced she came to say good-bye to him.

When I got home that night and walked through the door, I immediately knew what happened. I did not have to look at my husband—I just knew. I looked at my two dogs who came to greet me and then turned to my husband.

He looked at me and said, *"her heart just gave out"*.

She was buried by the time I got home, as John wanted to save me from the pain. That night I just lay there sobbing. I did not think that a person could have so many tears for as hard as I cried. We live on ten acres, and there is a creek that passes though our back yard. She was put to rest on the banks near the creek in a wooded area. I went early in the morning to where she was and picked a bouquet of wild black-eyed Susan's to place on her grave.

In my life I have had many blessings—I was born into a family who truly loved me and I married my best friend—my soul-mate. It is from these people that I have known the definition of love. However, I am also familiar with grief. I lost my mother when I was twenty, my father when I was twenty-seven and my brother to lung cancer when I was thirty. So, I am accustomed to sorrow and anguish as well, however, this particular experience caught me by surprise as its intensity was there with the rest of them.

The Saturday that the veterinarian diagnosed Snapper, John had gone to a car show. At that time John did not know the seriousness of her health. And as the saga of that week progressed, she inevitably did pass on. Well, after she died, he went to the car and brought me a stuffed little puppy with angel wings. He had purchased this stuffed animal at the car show. At that time none of us knew what was wrong with her, but we certainly did not expect her to die. I believe that this was a foreshadowing from the Universe, to possibly prepare both of us for what would eventually occur.

Our local newspaper ran an article on the memorial service that was held for the Kennedy and Bassette families. During the service Carolyn Kennedy's mother, Ann Freeman, read a part from Henry Scott Holland's meditation "Facts of Faith". I cut the article out and had it face outward on the inside of my curio cabinet. This is where my collection of ceramic dogs, Snapper's picture and the 'angel dog' are displayed. This passage got me through some very tough days. Every time I read it, I felt embraced by its depth for life and its profundity for death.

"Death is nothing at all. It does not count. I have slipped away into the next room…I am but waiting for you, for an interval, somewhere very near, just around the corner."

The area Snapper is buried is unspoiled and picturesque. We plan to plant some perennial bulbs that will bloom every year and install a swing set with a rose arbor. We would like to call this stretch of land 'Snapper's Garden' in memory of this special spirit who brought nothing but love in the short time she was here. We want this garden to be a place where one can come and remember their spirit. And although she is no longer with us, we hope that her passionate vibration for life will be encountered and passed on. Snapper's garden will be a place of rebirth.

I have concluded that although she had six years on this earth, I feel good about the time that she spent here. I was the first person to see her come into this world, to touch and pick her up, and the first person she ever licked. My husband John had the privilege to be the last to have ever held her before she went on. What struck me most about Snapper and how she affected my life was that she really knew nothing but love and how to love in her lifetime. She truly was a gift—just a divine presence to John and me.

Despite the sorrow, I am especially grateful to have known such unconditional love. Even though the sadness can often be jarring, I treasure what the Universe gave to me for six years—she was a lesson in love and that by itself is priceless. When Snapper passed on, I wrote to my brother saying that if humans aspired to have the kind of character and love that animals had, we would live in a completely different consciousness today. I am learning through Snapper's spirit what is the essence of unconditional love and non-judgment. I am learning to feel her wisdom in my surroundings.

This whole experience has been a lesson in faith. I think this was an ongoing lesson for all of us; at least it was for me. I do not think that there is ever an end to this lesson. I believe we go on and accept what we can't find rhyme or reason for, and trust that all will be revealed at the appropriate time. From the lesson of faith, we are given the gift of hope. In my case, the gift of hope was from Snapper via John…a black cocker spaniel puppy named Jitterbug. *"There is an appointed time for everything, and a time for every affair under the heavens".*

Thought 104

Money can be a rippling current, if we allow the tide to drift. However, this tide must evolve from the heart. Think about a time when you saw someone pan handling on the street. *What comes to mind?* Perhaps thoughts comparable to how able bodied they seem when begging; yet, somehow they cannot put that same energy into finding work. Or possibly you might think that they enjoy getting something for free. Whatever assumption one makes, we must try to put our self in the mind and body of that panhandler—if for only a minute.

We should look back to a time in our life when we felt the brunt of despair, whether it was emotional or financial. There was a time when we found ourselves needing the help of another. A few coins or dollars will not disrupt our budgets too badly. Furthermore, if given with the right intention, even if it is a humble amount, the laws of the universe come into play!

The love and sincerity transmitted from this amount creates a natural flow back in our direction. Only we must give for wanting, and not for needing, there is a difference. The slightest bit of apprehension will create a wall where the flow of prosperity will cease.

This does not mean that one is obligated to every panhandler or charity that requests a donation. When is it right to give and when does it become too much? Only we will know. Its consistency will sear our hearts and inflame our souls with certitude. We will feel an overwhelming sense of satisfaction and completion. This knowing-ness is our heart communicating to us— and the heart never lies.

Relationships, a Part of Who We Are

"Do all your duties, but keep your mind on God. Serve your wife, children, father, and mother; treat them as if they are very dear to you, but know in your heart that they do not belong to you."

Ramakrishna

Thought 105

All we have to depend on is the Self that resides within and the God we worship. We may be blessed with spouse, partner, and children in our lives, but in the end all we own is the essence of who we are. This essence is with us eternally.

Learning to become dependent on the divine Self will lessen the burden of anxiety and attachment. Our families are here for us to enjoy, nurture, and love. When control, or lack of identity is embedded in any relationship, the Self gradually begins to dissolve and detach.

When a loved one leaves the physical world or remains missing, it is then that we must realize that we came into this world alone, and will leave that same way. It is then that we actualize that we must put the same love, nurturing and dependency on the Self, as we did and continue to do with the ones we love on this plane.

So, in order for us to embody Self-love, we need to recognize that Self-centeredness must be applied. Centering on the Self will help us delve into a world where we will have the skills to cope and carry on. These mechanisms will be brought to us from unseen hands and just when we think we can't handle much more, a '*light worker*' will appear to help us further along our journey.

* * *

This is a story about a young man who had everything, and yet felt that he had nothing. This is a story of a mother who gave to everyone, but never to the Self within. There are no happy endings, nor substance for closure, and yet closure is found. Along this journey a mother who lived for her son—by loss and agony—found her Self.

This is the story of my brother Vijay:

For as long as I can remember, Vijay had the gift—the gift of turning nothing into something and something into gold—his nickname was the 'golden boy'. Whomever he met or whatever he did in his life—he was triumphant and well liked for it.

During his last year of high school, Vijay had decided he wanted to apply to a university in the States. His idea was not just any university—but either Princeton or Brown—both being Ivy Leagues. My parents were not in a position where they could afford such fees, and if Vijay were to be admitted, it would have to be on a scholarship. Applying as a foreign student and hoping to receive a scholarship seemed like a long shot—but he felt that he could get in and so he applied. Vijay was admitted to both Princeton and Brown on a scholarship due to his expertise in squash and scores on his SAT.

Vijay attended Brown University and was doing a double major in religion and biology while taking prerequisites for medicine. His interest in the religions of the world became more than just a curriculum. By his fourth year, he decided to do one semester at a local university where my parents lived, in St. Catherines, Ontario. It was here that we noticed he would stay up till the wee hours of the morning reading books on the various religions and their tenets. Vijay's philosophy was that all paths lead to One.

While he was attending Brown, Vijay met a girl, fell in love and subsequently wanted to marry her. Her faith was Moslem and her parents were against this relationship once they had found out its seriousness. When her parents told her to end it—she did. Vijay begged and pleaded for her to reconsider. He voiced to her that if religion was a problem, he would gladly convert. The answer was no. At the end of 1993, Vijay came to my house for Christmas. He was not looking his well self—and seemed to be in a state of anguish.

By January 1994, he went back to Brown University and after two weeks he called my father and told him that he wanted to come home. He said that he would finish up the last two courses in the spring session. When he came home, he told my dad that he wanted to make a trip to India, my father thought it was a great idea, as it would give him a chance to get to know his cousins and mother country. Brown University gave him permission to graduate in the spring with his class, provided that he took the two courses in the summer that would complete his degree.

Vijay went to Bombay where most of our family resides. In Bombay, Vijay's behavior became quite reclusive. He would eat very little and would sit and contemplate most of time. He went to Delhi to visit another of my father's sisters. From Delhi, he then went to Haridwar, a city north of India, that lays on the Ganges river. Many ashrams (spiritual hermitages) and religious groups reside in this city. Ashrams in India are places where anybody of any religion will be welcomed, and where food and shelter are provided for. It is a place where one finds their spirit.

Vijay went to several ashrams in Haridwar. At one in particular, he met a family where the mother was a well-known guru in the area that she came from, which was a town called Silchar in Assam, near the Himalayas.

I guess you can say that she had the gift of foresight, as she told him that he had two paths that could lead him down two very different roads. She said that if he were to go back to the west, he would become a great business man, however, if he should decide to come back to India, he would then become a great spiritual teacher. My brother left Haridwar back to Pune, where another aunt told my dad that she had noticed a significant change in his personality. He had become more withdrawn and would meditate for hours. During his stay at my aunt's in Pune, he made one last call to his girlfriend at Brown to see if she might have changed her mind. The answer remained the same; Vijay would leave India, only to return in a few weeks searching for an inner peace and truth beyond his comprehension.

He came back to my parent's place in St. Catherines, Ontario, and then went to Brown University to register for the upcoming semester. It was at Brown that he met her again and finalized in his own mind that there was no possible chance that they could share a life together. He came back to my parent's house and asked my dad whether he could go back to India. My dad said yes, however, he must finish the last two courses to his degree and then he could leave soon after, if he so desired.

Vijay had a month before the next semester would commence. He got a job where he had part stake in a health club in St. Catherines. He developed a pro shop and was the squash pro there. He saved up what he could in one month from the health club revenue. He then sold his hockey cards he collected as a child and raised about $1,000 dollars.

On Mother's Day, my father, mother and Vijay went out for dinner. At the restaurant, he did not eat anything and was making my father angry as he just stared into space. The next day a Monday, which was Victoria Day, Canada's national holiday, my dad had some family friends over. Vijay took their little daughter to the health club and then helped her with her math homework. When everyone had left, my dad found him lying on their bed. He asked him whether he wanted to come out with them for a drive. He did not respond, closed his eyes and continued lying there.

When they came back from the drive he was not there. They had just assumed that he went to his friend's place in Toronto and that he would return in the evening. He came late in the evening and my parents were both asleep. That very night he telephoned me in Pittsburgh and asked my husband if the tickets we bought for his graduation were refundable. We did not think much about the question and Vikram said no.

Tuesday morning, Vijay got up very early and left my parent's home. He did not return that night, so my parents assumed that he had slept at one of his friend's homes, which he often did in the past.

Wednesday morning, my mother went to her health club and was in the locker room when one of her friends came to her and said, *"I heard the your son went to India."*

My mother said, *"What? Tina, you are kidding, right?"*

Vijay had organized a boy's squash tournament at his health club and Tina's son was part of it. My mother went to where she and my dad always met for lunch and told him what had just transpired.

In those days, Air India's flights would leave only on Tuesday and Saturday. My dad told my mother that he must have left to India yesterday, which was Tuesday. At that point Vijay was using my mother's car and my mother had to find out where he left her vehicle. She went to his health club and asked if they knew where the car was. They said it was parked a few yards down. She found her car with the keys in the ignition and the doors unlocked.

The way his behavior was on his return from India, my father felt a certain relief that he was gone, as his quietude and anger made it uncomfortable for them. My parents found out later that Vijay's business partner, a married man with children of his own, had driven him to the airport. A few weeks later in June, my father received a letter from Vijay. It stated that he was in Silchar and that he would be traveling around to various ashrams in and around India. He wrote that he was going mad in the Western world, and that the peace he was seeking was here in the East. He went on to say that when his head becomes clear, he will then go to Pune, a city near Bombay and stay with my father's sister.

Every four to five months, a postcard or letter would be sent by him, conveying to us what he was doing in India but not where he was. After 1996, postcards were more infrequent, periodically coming after ten months. They stated that he was doing fine and not to worry about him as he was on a spiritual path.

In one of his letters he said, *"what I am doing most people think and talk about it, but conversely do nothing—one day—you will be proud of me."*

The path he partook in, to many would be called the journey of a sadhu (priest). This is when one gives up all connection to family and material life and seeks the path of enlightenment. Similar to what the Buddha did.

The last call my parents received was on December 31, 1996. They were in Australia at that time. He asked how everyone was keeping and said that he would call back. That was the last contact we had from him. My father tried to trace him out by the Indian military police in September 1997. My father had a friend who was a colonel in the army. Colonel Singh put two men on the case alongside himself and the three of them searched the various ashrams in the areas that Vijay had indicated in his letter. The people who ran the ashram in Silchar said that he was there but left. In India when one does not want to be found—one isn't.

Five and half years have passed since he left that Tuesday in May 1994—and although, at times the absence of his spirit is overwhelmingly painful, especially for my mother, something deeper has evolved through this process. My mother, who busied herself in raising the three of us, began to seek her mission in life. She tended to live through Vijay's esprit and energy. When he left, an immense part of who she was disappeared along with him.

At first she occupied herself with exercise classes at her health club and meeting friends occasionally. But gradually there came a point when this circumstance had to be faced head on and coped with. Two years after his departure, a slow painful process was embarked, which took her on an inward journey that surfaced a different set of talents and abilities. Walking into who she was, was something my mother rarely had time for, as the presence of the children, especially Vijay, engulfed her own sense of spirit and Self.

My mother began to realize that Vijay may or may not come back—but in order for her to survive mentally, emotionally, and spiritually, she had to find some sort of closure to an event that may never sanction closure. My mother sought out information on attending some health classes and enrolled herself at a local community college. She began to search the possibilities of getting a job. From the time she was married, she had worked for the duration of about three years, in the late eighties and early nineties, but nothing after.

So, at the age of fifty-nine she made an appointment to see a job counselor to become familiar with what she wanted to do with the rest of her life. Sue, the job counselor, told my mother that it was never too late to find a career that you love and have a passion for.

Together they narrowed the search to two areas my mother loved doing—one was counseling the elderly and the other was working with horticulture. For a period of about a year, my mother would see Sue, update her resume and attend seminars that the agency provided, while simultaneously applying to various places. She looked diligently for a job, knowing that it was never too late to find her true purpose, alongside being a mother and homemaker.

By April 1998, she was considered for a position in a home-care agency that was to open up within a month's time. She got the job and started working as a healthcare counselor. It has been seventeen months since she started and since then she has completed a patient service certificate in healthcare. She also received numerous letters and awards from her place of work, patients remarked on what a caring soul she was and how her essence brightened their day. Her patients refuse to have anyone else attend to them when my mother is on vacation or is sick. They waited for her to return.

Although what happened to our family could be explained as karmic, something that each one of us had to experience; each soul on this earth incarnates not only to handle and learn from our karma—but to also serve and contribute to this planet. My mother did so by creating symmetry and balance in the souls of her sick patients. This tranquility was harvested by way of the healing words in which she voiced and the healing touch in which she imparted.

A short addendum to this story comes from me to them—Vijay's sister. I believe what has struck me the most since my brother's sudden departure, is that we are not so much in control of life as we think we are, and that learning to *really* and *truly* surrender to the divine is one of life's most painstaking lessons.

However, I think the most arduous of all lessons is realizing that the loved ones in our life do not belong to us, they never have and they never will. They are a gift for us to realize our strengths and weaknesses, to overcome certain karmic patterns whether good or bad, and then for us to continue on in this world by fulfilling the mission we set out to do when we incarnated on this planet. Vijay's gift to my family was introspection of the Divine Self within each of us. We came to know that we were stronger than we thought and we came to learn the meaning of letting-go.

Thought 106

People touch our lives in different ways. Sometimes a person may come into our life for a short period of time and we may be left to wonder what ever happened to that relationship. One should not be concerned by the loss but rather, focus on the connection that was developed and what was acquired from its existence. If for some reason the relationship ceased, it is because there was no longer a need for it.

In that particular time, it may have been necessary for learning, karma, and growth, but now its duration has expired, leaving only the affair of its wisdom. It is within these walls of experience that one must reflect, master, and release the relationship, regardless of its positive or negative residues.

Thought 107

The West cherishes the voice of the young; while the East has a more difficult time engaging their youth to freely deliberate or question elders and professors. Rather, to do so would illustrate some degree of disrespect. The West, however, encourages their young minds to question, debate and most of all understand that their opinion is valued, heard, and respected—despite their age. While in the East, age symbolizes wisdom, as young voices are sometimes overshadowed. The West celebrates independent thinking and creates individualization in their young minds!

Nonetheless, the Western general attitude towards the elderly differs to some extent. A substantial number of seniors tend to live somewhat lonely isolated lives (not all of course). The older one is, the less noticed are their voice and purpose. Generally speaking, in most Eastern cultures, considerable respect is endowed to the aging, as their ascension to wisdom is claimed through the maturing process. Rarely are they isolated; involvement and respect is embodied by most Eastern families where a frame of mind is carried from generation to generation. The responsibility bequeathed to the young is of love and duty.

The cultural differences seen within both hemispheres demonstrate how East and West can learn from across each others' ocean.

Thought 108

Age and experience is one of life's true paradoxes. One can be sixty and have learned very little from their sixty years on Earth, and yet one can be a quarter of that age and had a lifetime's worth of experience, knowledge, and mastery. Do not discriminate because age equates judgment and wisdom.

There are many individuals whose experience and maturity are beyond their chronological years and have achieved a level of Self-mastery that one has yet to see in some adults.

Learn that our teachers come to us in many forms and of varying ages. We must learn to become aware. Do not close your mind off to another because you feel your adulthood has earned you a level of learnedness. Insight and wisdom are a state of consciousness and rarely of time.

Thought 109

We are meant in some way to have a teacher, someone to guide us through life's innate pathway. This presence will come to us only when we are ready. It will be the Master who will find us, not the other way around.

Once the light within us becomes realized—its shimmer will attract the Master with whom we are connected to. This is formulated via our *inner dimensions.* This may manifest through a book that we happen to pick up, from a conversation we happen to hear,or from a situation we find ourselves in.

However its appearance, it is made known through the non-physical dimensions first, before it influences and manifests outwardly—these dimensions are the inner planes of life. This initiates the path of our pilgrimage—the pilgrimage of truth.

* * *

This story is about finding our spiritual path and the relationship between a Realized Master/Guru and their student. I met Linda through a mutual friend of ours and since, we have become friends.

Her devotion to God has enlightened me on what it literally means to surrender without attachment and to surrender without fear. I am honored to share her story.

This is Linda's story:

I am a psychotherapist by profession. One of my job responsibilities at a previous place of employment was to develop educational programs on a college campus. It was National Collegiate Alcohol Awareness Week and I was looking for someone to give a talk on adult children of alcoholics. The woman I had in mind to give this presentation could not do it, so I ended up calling another woman at a local chemical dependency treatment center. I used to work with her and had been wanting to call her since I heard she made a trip to India. We scheduled to meet, as she agreed to give the talk. My curiosity for

India had heightened and I was feeling compelled to learn all I could about this country. I met her at a coffee shop and she told me about her visit to an ashram (hermitage) where a holy man lives.

I was so enthralled in hearing about India that suddenly I blurted out, *"Maria, can I go with you on your next trip?"*

I did not know Maria very well to ask her such a question, but I felt such an earnest desire to go at that moment. She did not jump on it. She told me to read Autobiography of a Yogi and the Self-Realization Fellowship lessons by Paramahansa Yogananda (Saint and Realized Master).

In December 1995, Maria took me to a healing retreat center in Michigan where they have various workshops and teachings on meditation, healing, yoga, etc. It is a Yogananda Center. I was introduced to the guru/disciple relationship while staying there. I had a powerful spiritual experience that weekend and was becoming more familiar with my inner world. In July 1996, I was invited to a womens' gathering at Maria's friend's home. Pam invited both of us to go to India with her in January 1997. Maria and Pam had made the journey together previously. When Pam asked me, I began crying. Something really was touching my heart very deeply inside! I didn't fully understand it at the time. I had no idea how I would finance the trip or who would care for my daughter—I just knew in my heart that I was meant to go to India. Before leaving Pam's house, she gave me vibhuti (holy ash) that came from the holy man's ashram in India. I learned that in India, vibhuti is as sacred as what we in the West call holy water.

Maria got married and was not able to make the journey to India with Pam and me. At that time, I did not know Pam very well, but I liked her and felt comfortable making the trip with her. My desire to meet this holy man was increasing. Pam had given me a book about him. His name is Sri Sathya Sai Baba. I was beginning to make a connection with him through his teachings, which made a lot of sense to me. I now needed to ask for some time off from work. I had time accumulated, but I needed three weeks in a row off and I was afraid they would not permit it. I asked my boss if I could take the three weeks in order that I could travel abroad. He told me this it was not possible. I went to my office and started praying about what I should do. I continued praying for a few days and asked God to give me some clarity. I finally decided that I was going to quit my job so that I could make the trip to India. I was at a juncture in my life where I felt that my spirituality was much more important than my job. I have a Master's degree in Social Work; I thought that if I could not find another professional position, I would work two minimum wage jobs to support my daughter and myself upon my return. I decided that going to India was too important. I knew in my heart that this trip was going to be a turning point in my life and I felt that I would leave it in God's hands.

That same week, I received a phone call from a friend who I used to work with. They had an opening at the agency she was working at. This happened so fast that it seemed that the Divine was giving me the confirmation I needed to leave this job and go to India. For me to consider taking the new position, my friend conveyed to her boss that I would need to take three weeks off in January to go out of the country. I was offered the job with that condition. Within a week and a half, I quit my job, interviewed for the other job and was offered the position making $7,000.00 more than I was currently making, and was seriously making arrangements to visit India.

It seemed like the moment I said, *"God, I will quit this job so I can go to India, because my spirituality takes precedence over any work",* everything flowed into rhythm.

Once I sincerely surrendered, everything instantaneously began falling into place. The path was made clear. My focus now was on going to India. I was able to work extra and make money for the trip. My daughter stayed with her father.

When we got to the ashram, I did not know what to expect at all. I had no idea, but I trusted and had faith that God was in charge of what would happen to me. I went to darshan (blessing and sight of a holy being) for the first time and it was then that I knew I was home. I cried; it really touched my heart. It was as if I did not have to move from this spot for the rest of my life. Something touched me inside and I felt that I could have stayed there. I realized that experiencing Sai Baba's presence and divine love were what I had been searching for my entire life.

Soon into the first darshan, I began having my own inner experiences. When I was in the darshan area, I felt illuminated by light that seemed to be all over. It did not matter what was going on around me. This experience was occupying my consciousness internally. It was something that I had never experienced previously. Each time I went in for darshan, I felt that Sai Baba's presence was connecting me closer with God. Each darshan filled me more with the totality of Spirit and I felt my energy shifting. His aura was startling and his presence was beyond words. This holy man truly emanated a being close to divinity.

There was a tremendous amount of synchronicity occurring on the ashram daily. The lessons I had been trying to figure out for years would be answered in one day. It was as if the light finally clicked on. Being in the ashram was a life changing experience for me. I felt that I had made a real connection to Sai Baba as my teacher and guru. He continues to bring me closer to God. My experiences at Prasanthi Nilayam (name of ashram) made me realize at my inner most core that God is really everything. And that God comes through to us by way of other people and by way of other divine beings.

When I prayed to God before, I was basically praying to the Universe, to that energy source. By connecting with Sai Baba, God was giving me a clearer direction, specific teachings and an avenue to become closer to Him. In my mind, I needed something more specific. I knew that Sai Baba was my representation of a divine being and my link to strengthening my relationship with the divine.

Some people have a guru whom they spend time with daily, like Irina Tweedie in her book, Daughter of Fire. I have been to India to see Sai Baba only twice. One does not have to spend time in the physical presence of their teacher. The relationship really occurs on a spiritual plane, the same as a person's relationship with God or Higher Power. The language we communicate through is divine love. It is a heart experience. Before I knew Baba, I knew God in my head. Now that I know Baba, he has taught me to experience and know God in my heart.

I want to convey that having a teacher or guru is obtainable to anyone who has this sincere desire in his heart. The guru is your spiritual teacher, a special teacher whom you have a one-on-one relationship with. One does not have to travel to India to find a guru.

The guru finds you. Open your heart; be very serious and sincere on your spiritual path. Be disciplined in following your spiritual practices (meditation, prayer, chanting, listening to devotional music, attending service, reading spiritual literature, serving others, etc.). Pray for your teacher to come to you and stay open. Trust that it will happen at the right time. When the student is ready, the teacher appears.

Sai Baba's messages are about God, spiritual truths, and how interconnected we all are to each other. He has taught me the universality of all religions. In his ashram, there is representation of Christianity, Islam, Shin-to, Buddhism, Hinduism, Sikhism, Judaism, Jainism, Taoism, and Confucianism. Sai Baba has taught me about selfless love, selfless service, nonattachment, and devotion to the divine. My consciousness has changed and I am forever grateful to be aware of the subtleties that life brings to me daily.

The divine in you connects with the divine in the teacher and in time, the teacher brings you up to his level. You learn according to your level of consciousness. The lessons get deeper spiritually as you progress. It is like being in school; the lessons become harder as you move up to the higher grade levels. However, each grade passed prepares you for the next level of learning and experiences. Having a guru/disciple relationship is like having your own special tutor, personally assigned to you by whatever supreme power you believe in. Your program is tailor made for your own soul's growth.

One needs to really check out ones potential guru before one accept him to make sure, without any doubts, that he is the right one for you to follow. Take it very seriously and question their credentials. Your relationship with the divine is the most important relationship in your life, whichever path you follow.

And in the end, it is the relationship and how you feel with your teacher and the divine that is most significant. You know this in your soul and it doesn't matter what anyone thinks or says. What is of substance is your soul's evolution and remembering who you really are.

About the Author

Samira Rao would like to hear from you. If you're interested in receiving information on a forthcoming *"Living in Chaos is Living in Stability"* newsletter please write or email her.

Samira Rao
P.O. Box 513
Grand Blanc, Michigan 48439

Website address: www.samirarao.net
Email address: samirarao@yahoo.com

Glossary

1. Ashram - a spiritual hermitage, or monastery.

2. Astral Body - man's subtle body of light or prana, the second of three sheaths which encase the soul.

3. Astral World - The Lord's creation of a subtle sphere comprised of light and color. Every being, object, and vibration on the material plane has its counterpart in the astral plane. The astral is the blueprint of the physical world and is only a breath away.

4. Atman - The Self, the Soul, the Absolute, the Divinity that resides above and beyond the mind, body, and intellect.

5. Avatar - An incarnation of God, a Divine being manifest in human form.

6. Bhagavad Gita - means the "Song of the Lord". Ancient Indian scriptures consisting of eighteen chapters from the Mahabharata epic. Teachings of the avatar Krishna to his disciple Arjuna.

7. Brahman - The universal absolute existence, un-nameable and beyond description; the transcendent God-head.

8. Chakras - The seven Yogic centers of Consciousness.

9. Consciousness - Four states of consciousness: the waking state, the sleeping state, the dreaming state, and the super-conscious state.

10. Dharma - Universal truth, duty, righteousness.

11. Esoteric - Inner world, the spiritual world.

12. Exoteric - Outer world, the physical world.

13. Karma - Action and reaction, cause and affect, sowing and reaping. Every human becomes the master of his own destiny by his thoughts and actions, past, present and future.

14. Kurma Nadi - Energy that begins at the base of the spine and radiates up to the throat. Functions as stabilizer of mind and body.

15. Light worker - evolved soul working on Earth.

16. Mantra - A sacred verse or name of God.

17.Maya - Illusion.

18. Nirvana - Where there is no wind: Enlightenment, Bliss, Ecstasy, Completion.

19. Prana - The vital breath force of life. Thought energies of God which are substances of the astral plane and a primal energy from which all mental and physical energy evolves from in the physical world.

20. Prema - Unconditional love, universal love, love of the Self.

21. Puga - A ceremony pertaining to religious beliefs and customs.

22. Sai - Divine mother of all.

23. Sadhu— Holy man

24. Samadhi—Consciousness merges with the Cosmic Spirit and mind is unwavering and tranquil, state of super-conscious eighth step in raja yoga (royal path) as outlined by the sage Patangali.

25. Sannyasin - A monk who has taken the final vows of renunciation.

26. Sathya - Divine unchanging truth.

27. Seva - Service to Self, family, and community

28. Super-Consciousness - Known also as Christ consciousness or cosmic consciousness, this state is experienced in meditation where one removes the I and realizes the Self.

29. Swami - A spiritual teacher, monk or sannyasin.

30. Upanishads - A sacred scripture which forms the knowledge portion of the Vedas.

31. Vedas - The ancient Scriptures of Hindu thought dated back to 2500 B.C.. There are four scriptural texts: Rig Veda, Sama Veda, Yajur Veda, and Atharva Veda.

32. Vedanta - Religious philosophical principles which has evolved from the Vedas; it is one of the six systems of Hindu thought. The essential concept of Vedanta is that Truth is One, men and women in their essential nature are Divine, and the goal is to realize their Divinity, whichever path they choose.

Suggested Readings

"A part of who I am lies astir within each of these teachings. Subsequently, these truths have become a part of my life...a part of my prana."

Samira Rao

Carlson Richard. Don't Sweat The Small Stuff...and it's all small stuff. New York, New York: Hyperion, 1997.

Chinmoy Sri. Yoga and the Spiritual Life. Jamaica, New York: Aum Publications, 1996

Chopra Deepak. The Seven Spiritual Laws Of Success. San Rafael California: Amber-Allen Publishing and New World Library, 1994.

Chopra Deepak. The Way Of The Wizard. New York, New York: Random House, 1995.

Mark, Barbara and Griswold Judy. Angelspeake: A Guide to Talk With Your Angels.
New York, New York: Simon & Shuster, 1995.

Mata Daya, Sri. Finding The Joy Within You. Los Angeles, California: Self Realization Fellowship, 1990.

Myss, Caroline. Energy Anatomy (Audio Tape) U.S.A. 1996

Myss, Caroline. Why People Don't Heal And How They Can. (Audio Tape) U.S.A:
Mountain Drive, Faust Entertainment., and CineMedia Corp, 1997

Roof, Jonathan. Pathways To God: A Study Guide To The Teaching Of Sathya Sai Baba. Faber, Virginia: Leela Press Inc., 1991.

Vaughan-Lee Llewellyn. Sufism: Transformation of the Heart. Inverness, California:

The Golden Sufi Center, 1995.

ViveKananda Swami. Vedanta: Voice of Freedom. New York, New York: Philosophical Library, 1998.

Walsch, Neale. Conversations with God Book 1. New York, New York: G.P. Putnam's Sons 1996.

Walsch, Neale. Conversations with God Book 3. Charlottesville, VA: Hampton Roads Publishing Company, Inc. 1998.

Yogananda Paramahansa. Man's Eternal Quest. Los Angeles, California: Self Realization Fellowship, 1982.

Zukav, Gary. The Seat Of The Soul. New York, New York: Fireside, 1990.

Bibliography

Bruce, Rita. Vision of Sai: Book 1. York Beach, Maine. Samuel Weiser, INC., 1995.

Chibhavananda Swami. Daily Divine Digest. Tirupparaitturai, India: Sri Ramakrishna
Tapovanom, 1974.

Chinmoy, Sri. Yoga and the Spiritual Life. Jamaica, New York: Aum Publications, 1996

Harrison, Gavin. In the Lap Of The Buddha. Boston, Massachusetts: Shambhala
Publications, 1994.

Davis, Eugene. With God. Lakemont, Georgia: Center for Spiritual Awareness, 1995.

Lorie, Peter & Mascetti Dunn. The Quotable Spirit. Great Britain: New Leaf, 1996.

Mandelkorn Philip. To Know Your Self. United States: Integral Yoga Publications, 1988.

Vaughan-Lee Llewellyn. Sufism: Transformation of the Heart. Inverness, California:
The Golden Sufi Center, 1995.

End Note

"My heart is open to all forms; it is a pasture for gazelles and a monastery for Christian monks a temple for idols and the Ka'bah for the pilgrim The tables of the Torah and The book of the Koran. Mine is the religion of Love Wherever His caravans turn, the religion of Love shall be my religion And my faith".

Ibn 'Arabi

Printed in the United States
4631